TRANSFORM *BURNED OUT* INTO *CHILLED OUT!*

The Art of *Chilling Out* for Women

100+ Ways to Replace Worry and Stress with Spiritual Healing, Self-Care, and Self-Love

Angela D. Coleman

Adams Media
New York   London   Toronto   Sydney   New Delhi

Adams Media
An Imprint of Simon & Schuster, Inc.
100 Technology Center Drive
Stoughton, Massachusetts 02072

First Adams Media hardcover edition April 2023

ADAMS MEDIA and colophon are trademarks of Simon & Schuster.

For information about special discounts for bulk purchases, please contact Simon & Schuster Special Sales at 1-866-506-1949 or business@simonandschuster.com.

The Simon & Schuster Speakers Bureau can bring authors to your live event. For more information or to book an event contact the Simon & Schuster Speakers Bureau at 1-866-248-3049 or visit our website at www.simonspeakers.com.

Interior design by Julia Jacintho
Interior images © 123RF/Rungrote Sae-kueng

Manufactured in China

10 9 8 7 6 5 4 3 2 1

Library of Congress Cataloging-in-Publication Data has been applied for.

ISBN 978-1-5072-1993-5
ISBN 978-1-5072-1994-2 (ebook)

DEDICATION

Above all, this book is dedicated to you, the reader. I appreciate that you purchased this book to invest in yourself, and I honor your journey. *Asé!*

ACKNOWLEDGMENTS

Thank you to my Ancestors, my biological and spiritual family, for giving me life, strength, and beauty. Their grace, love, support, guidance, blessings, and protections carry me every day in every way.

Thank you to my teachers and friends, my tribe that I can count on to love me unconditionally and completely no matter what, those who know how to live a great life, love, serve, and enjoy what's here without compromising who they are.

Thank you to my furry tortie companion, Princess, for being good company everywhere I worked and wrote, and for being bossy when it was time to take a break.

Finally, I would like to thank my daughter, Ayana, a beautiful flower who motivates and inspires me each day to try new things and be my best self.

CONTENTS

Part Two:

MIND...85

Part Three:
SPIRIT...153

APPENDIX...230

INDEX...234

INTRODUCTION

"Almost everything will work again if you unplug it for a few minutes, including you."

—Anne Lamott

Feeling worried? Overworked? Burned out? Are you hiding those feelings behind a storm of busyness that's just causing even more stress? If this sounds like you, you are not alone. In a world where women are more worn out than ever before, this stress can lead to serious mental and physical consequences. To break this vicious cycle, you need to learn to relax…and chill out.

With *The Art of Chilling Out for Women*, you'll learn to prioritize yourself and transform from a stressed-out worrier to a relaxation warrior. Here you'll find 101 practical tips that will help you release that tension, process the stressors in your life, and even derive benefit from them. Using the universal principles of tried-and-true traditional customs practiced by countless cultures around the world, the sustainable, down-to-earth survival strategy of chilling out is applicable to just about everyone at any time. This book will walk you through the steps that will put you on the path to a better life. You'll find affirmations that will boost your confidence, herbs and gemstones that will help put you in the right frame of mind for chilling out, and even ways to use feng shui to keep your environments more calm and peaceful. With the help of this book, you can make chilling out on a regular basis your new normal. This is the best way to live.

With a diversity of applications, chilling out includes powerful moments of self-exploration, self-awareness, and self-discovery. The key is knowing that you *can*. Do it anytime. Any place. This is your moment to…chill out. Let it go and be who you are supposed to be with no filter, no apologies.

HOW TO USE THIS BOOK

The Art of Chilling Out for Women is a guide for healthy behavior—self-help at its very best! Like a doctor writes a prescription for medicine when you need additional help for an illness, I created this book as a nonmedical prescription to optimize your health and healing.

With a medical prescription, you still have to go to the doctor, fill it at the drugstore, and take the medication regularly to get better. Some people might call this "doing the work." Whether you receive holistic prescriptions from me or medical ones from your doctor, nothing works if you don't do the work. But instead of thinking of it as "work," let's look at it as service to yourself, or self-care.

Chilling out may be a challenge for you. A big change. Just know that greater self-awareness helps you act with more precision and impact. You probably already realized that something is off-balance with you. With *The Art of Chilling Out for Women*, you have what you need to find your inner balance again, but you still must be willing to do the work. Don't worry! There is detailed knowledge and motivation in this book, plus helpful tips in the Holistic Prescription sections at the end of each entry. Read on to learn how to use *The Art of Chilling Out for Women* to your maximum benefit.

MAKING SELF-CARE A PRIORITY

Your healthy lifestyle starts with a strong desire to love and prioritize yourself, followed by behaviors that are consistent with this desire. Ask yourself, "Does this action serve my highest good?" If you stay focused and on task, it may be much simpler than you realize. *The Art of Chilling Out for Women* will show you how. When you focus on self-care, you give yourself permission to stop trying to be Superwoman. You can take your need for self-care, peace, and relaxation to the next level through the specific actions outlined in each of the entries in this book.

THE HOLISTIC ATTITUDE

We all have a physical body, influenced by the mind, led by our spirit. It's a united, even synergistic, process in which one undoubtedly affects the other. That is why we use the word *holistic*. It means that the prescriptions in each entry consider the interconnected, whole person.

Everything is holistic: your job, your home, your business, your relationships. Our remedies must reflect this reality, too, which is why I call them Holistic Prescriptions. This book is divided into three parts—body, mind, and spirit—to simplify the process. Part 1: Body shows you how to make changes in your physical self. Part 2: Mind shows you how to change the way you think and process information. Part 3: Spirit shows you the way through Spirit—your soul and inner guide. With this design, you can pick your focus to be what you need to achieve optimal chill for a healthier, worry-free lifestyle.

In concert with these three parts, each entry contains specific, strategic recommendations to help you on your journey, which we will discuss in just a bit. They are:

- Affirmations
- Calls to Action
- Mother Nature
- Gemstones
- Feng Shui

Because the body, mind, and spirit are all connected, making changes to your body has an impact on your mind and spirit. Your body and spirit can be altered with your mind. Similarly, making changes to your spirit can change your body and mind. Let's discuss each of these parts in a bit more detail.

Body

The body is typically what you can see and understand most clearly. Feelings like pain and pleasure are easily distinguished. If you hit your knee on a wooden table, you feel pain. It hurts and might even leave a mark. Because of that experience, you learn not to do it again.

Most of us are familiar with the body because this is something emphasized in our everyday lives. Women's bodies, in particular, are often objectified, judged, and controlled. In fact, it could be said that we place too much emphasis on the body and not enough on the mind and spirit. The body is important but still part of the whole.

Your body tells you that when it is afraid, when it is fighting something, you are in distress. Anxiety makes your heart beat faster, and you might start to sweat. A stressful event might trigger a headache. Long-term imbalance may produce a tumor or another indication of disease. You just want the indicator of disease to be gone and disappear for good, but first it will be helpful to know the source. By resolving the issue at the source, you can prevent and resolve distress or dis-ease in the body. In the entries about the body, you will learn how to read your body barometers, take back your energy, protect your heart, use natural healing, absorb joy and gratitude, beautify your life, soothe yourself, and much more.

Mind

Most people think that the mind is the most powerful part of a human being. Clearly, our minds are powerful. We can create a peaceful space using only our minds to meditate ourselves into this realm. However, it does not function by itself. If your body is the barometer, your soul is the compass, and the mind is the engine.

Looking out for yourself, acting in your own best interest, and being healthy is not always intuitive, especially after years of social conditioning to do the opposite. Your mind is a great asset in helping you undo the false narratives and change how you move forward.

Your mind can be the tool to get you going to help your body exist in wellness. If it is rational and perceptive, it will help you organize your activities around your goals. Attraction, retention, intention—the mind is at work here too. Your mind can also help you create much-needed space. A space to renew, recharge, vent, and be yourself is not optional. We all need it, and some of us need it badly. You can spend time here alone or with caring confidantes. The point is, you can be who you really are here. In the entries about the mind, you will learn how to stop living in chaos, parent yourself, accept change, let go of the past, overcome blind spots, go next-level, daydream, and use your mind in many other ways to achieve things that you may not have thought possible.

Spirit

When you practice spending your time in safe spaces, your mind expands too. You are creating a lifestyle of wellness and stress management. It is a natural phenomenon with amazing results. But... you don't need to go anywhere—there is no need to visit a church, Buddhist temple, or African shrine to get your daily fix!

Spirit is the foundation of our existence. If we are tuned into it, it will tell our body and mind exactly what to do. But, over the years, most of us have become so disconnected from our spirit and so inundated with external influences that we often override our spirit's wisdom and intentions with our intellectual minds; instead of allowing our physical bodies to be led with our spirit, we tell our bodies what to do with our minds.

Chilling out promotes realignment with your spiritual self by providing space between you and your activities. After chilling out, you can take the breaks that you were always intended to take. These breaks allow your spirit to shine instead of being smothered or hidden in the shadows.

The entries about Spirit are designed to help you regain your strength, power, and wisdom by reconnecting and listening more closely to Spirit, encouraging you to let go of your baggage (physical, mental, and psychic) and make choices that feed your soul without guilt, feelings of self-indulgence, or Fear of Missing Out (FOMO). In this part of the book, you will learn how to consistently choose peace, stay grounded, create a protective shield, listen to and nurture your soul, connect to Spirit, become a force of nature, find your Spot, overcome loneliness, cleanse, and have no fear. Of course, there's more, too, and it's exciting, game-changing stuff. In this way, *The Art of Chilling Out for Women* can positively impact how you view yourself and live your life.

Affirmation

Each entry in this book contains an affirmation. An *affirmation* is a positive statement phrased in the present that affirms who you are—and it is my favorite form of positive self-talk. You can say an affirmation aloud or quietly in your head—the point is to say it and believe it! Affirmations help ground you in your present reality and give you much-needed perspective. It's interesting how what we say to ourselves, both positive and negative, can and will affect us.

When you are having a hard time, do you put yourself down or lift yourself up? Whose voice is coming up when you hear that self-talk? Is that voice truly your own or is it your mother's, your father's, a teacher's, or someone else's? Who are they to you, and why has their voice become your voice?

Use affirmations to silence self-criticism and doubt. With positive self-talk, you can affirm your unique gifts to maintain self-love, self-care, and self-preservation in your quest to relax and let go. The Affirmation section of each entry of this book provides a specific affirmation for making the most of your active mind to maximize your life experiences.

The more you incorporate affirmations into your daily life, the more natural they will become, seamlessly migrating from an external process to an internal one; your enlightened outer voice becomes your enlightened inner voice. When you are having trouble putting yourself first, affirmations help you bring the focus back to what's most important: *you.*

You can say affirmations at any time. Some women find it helpful to create a habit of stating affirmations when they brush their teeth in the morning or when retiring for the evening. State your chosen affirmation aloud in the morning, at night, when you are in distress and in need, or when you are relaxed and at peace. Affirmations are always helpful, all the time.

Holistic Prescription

The affirmations in this book will keep you on track, and the *holistic prescriptions* will help you perfect your process. The Holistic Prescription in each entry helps you get started with a call to action, select natural herbal remedies for healing, choose gemstones to activate for the situation you are facing, and benefit from the practice of feng shui.

Call to Action

We often have no time set aside for ourselves. The shifts never end, and the expectations we have for ourselves can be even greater than the ones imposed upon us by others. This pattern has to change. Being everything for everybody is impossible. Trying to do it is a recipe for fatigue and disease. There's a far more effective, gentler solution. And it requires a whole lot less effort. It's called *chilling out*. Chilling out means *being there for yourself*. Sometimes, to do this, all you need is a little motivation to get started. Sometimes you need a *call to action*.

To change your situation for the long term, you must change your behavior. However, before you get anxious about following a strict set of rules and regulations, know this: Behavioral changes do not have to be severe or disruptive to be effective. In fact, if they are easy to do and enjoyable, they become long-lasting habits that are easily incorporated into your wellness lifestyle. This is one of the main objectives.

The Call to Action section of each entry includes a simple, yet significant behavioral shift to meet the goal of the entry. This is the first step you need to take to chill out, slow down, and release busyness to increase your overall well-being.

 Mother Nature

Plants such as herbs and flowers are natural healing substances. That is why I recommend all-natural scents for healing and self-expression. The closer to the source, the better. Herbal remedies, including aromatherapy, have withstood the test of time. They are ancient and effective.

Herbs

The Mother Nature section of each entry includes herbs and other plants to benefit your healing journey. You'll learn what each herbal remedy is good for and how it can help with the problem at hand. But there are so many ways to use herbs, so where do you start? Let's begin with the different methods. There are many options for using natural herbs; choose the technique that suits you best.

- **Burning:** Burn herbs on a piece of charcoal in a fireproof container.
- **Ingesting:** Use herbs in cooking or brew them into a tea to serve hot or cold, in capsules, dried, fresh, or as a tincture.
- **Soaking:** Put herbs in your bathwater for soaking into your skin and muscles.
- **Spraying:** Put herbs in a spray bottle with distilled water to make an herbal spritz.
- **Placing:** Put herbs in a sachet in your drawer, in a bowl on a table, or anywhere you wish to smell them.
- **Smoke cleansing:** Roll herbs together to form an herbal stick or bundle, light one end, and allow the smoke to waft over yourself and your environment.
- **Rubbing:** Add essential oils, herbs, and carrier oils together to use as a body oil.

Scents

Scents can be powerfully uplifting. The science of using plants and oils for health and healing is called *aromatherapy*. You don't have to be a scientist to use what you are attracted to and what makes you feel good. Allow your creativity to shine here using nature's bounty. Of course, there are many ways to experience scents—let your imagination run wild! However, when you feel the need to relax and let go, consider these proven aromatherapy solutions:

- Perfumes
- Lotions
- Candles
- Incense
- Oils

- Food
- Plants
- Beverages
- Baths
- Flowers

Gemstones

Crystals, minerals, and gems are natural, portable healing stones. Gemstones are beautiful, small, and mighty. Do you feel them vibrate when you hold them in your hand? One of Mother Nature's many precious gifts, they come in all shapes, colors, and densities. They deserve your respect and should not be underestimated. The Gemstones section of each entry suggests specific gemstones that will help with the issue being discussed. You will learn what each gemstone is best for, so you can pick and choose the ones that make sense for you.

There are many ways to use crystals and gemstones to your benefit. Metaphysical, scientific, and just plain awesome, the capabilities of gemstones have no limits when it comes to energy: They can receive it, manipulate it, store it, release it, transform it, reflect it, magnify it, redirect it, transfer it, organize it, balance it, and more.

When you hold specific stones and crystals with intention, you activate them—this is mind, body, and spirit in action! Although you do not always "see" this activity, you will feel it. Here are some tips:

- Cleanse your gemstones before your first use by rinsing them with seawater or salt water, or by placing them in sunlight or moonlight.
- Use gemstones by holding them in your hands and communicating your intention.

- Place gemstones near you, like on your nightstand at bedtime, under your pillow before sleeping, or on your desk when working.
- Carry gemstones in your pocket or purse.
- If you want to get more fancy, you can set gemstones in jewelry or place them on corresponding chakra areas of your body to stimulate those areas.

There are countless ways to use gemstones, so do your research and rely on your intuition to guide you.

 Feng Shui

Feng shui is the ancient Chinese practice of balancing your space to align with the harmony of the laws of nature, specifically the five elements: water, wood, earth (soil), metal, and fire. It has been practiced in Egypt, India, other parts of Asia, and around the world. Simply put, we all have an emotional energy field around our bodies. Sometimes, our energy field clashes with the spaces around us; other times, it fits right in. Feng shui respects and responds to this energy.

Love, energy, joy, healing—they all reside here. Pain, stagnation, and negativity can be here too. That is why our home environment is so important to our well-being. Health and happiness can be increased by maintaining harmony and vibrancy in our immediate environment and personal spaces.

The Feng Shui section of each entry includes practices that will provide optimal feng shui balance and harmony. It takes consciousness to be aware of the elements around you and how much of one thing can throw it out of whack. Earth, air, water, and fire; chi; yin and yang; furniture placement; plants; energy centers in the home; health and wealth centers… Your study and use of feng shui can go as deep as you want to get with it.

IT'S TIME TO CHILL OUT

Maybe you had difficulties with meditation in the past. Maybe you have trouble accepting change. Maybe you believe metaphysical explanations are a bit woo-woo and not for you. It doesn't matter. Your path is clear, and the work that you need to do is right in front of you. Your blessings are fully supported. All you have to do is call them to action.

Whether you are a beginner and have never put any of these concepts into action before, a seasoned professional looking to move to the next level in your self-development, or somewhere in-between, *The Art of Chilling Out for Women* is for you. Never stop. Keep going. The journey never ends. Maybe this part of your beautiful and endless journey is just the new beginning you've been waiting for.

Part One

BODY

Do you sometimes work very hard, only to be spinning your wheels? If so, you may feel like you are moving in place, lacking progress. Your body is off-balance and showing signs of distress. You don't have to do that. This doesn't have to be your life.

Due to a modern lifestyle that prioritizes work over rest, chilling out has become a lost art, a forgotten science. We need to bring it back in order to save ourselves.

Your mind and spirit function best when your body is at peace. Balanced equilibrium is your instinctual resting place. Your body is the mechanism by which you get things done. It's your body. Do what you want to do with it. But first, please *respect* it.

When your body wants to chill out, why not obey? It needs to restore and reset itself. Part 1 will show you how to do just that—by investing in yourself, absorbing joy and gratitude, getting restorative rest, creating a heart-filled life, and implementing many more techniques!

Learn to listen to what your body wants and needs to optimize your health and emotional well-being. It's a wonderful creation. Listen to what it is telling you. Take care of it. Nurture it. And be kind to it.

1

DISCOVER YOUR BODY BAROMETERS

How you respond to situations is rooted deep in your personal history. These are your *body barometers*.

Fight or flight. It's our survival mechanism. When you are triggered by something, your nervous system goes into overdrive. The stress hormones (cortisol, adrenaline, epinephrine, and norepinephrine) are all activated to help your body power through stressful situations. But if you are "on" all the time, trapped in a constant state of heightened awareness and stress, you can physically suffer. It can be a lonely and exhausting experience.

What happens to your body in this state? You might perspire and even feel nauseous. Stress headaches are common, as are stomachaches because your digestion can also be affected. But hold on. Breathe and chill for a few.…You don't have to fight anyone or go anywhere.

To understand your body barometers, learn what your body does under distress and why it does it. Your physical response is not a bad thing. It's your body's awesome and amazing way of protecting you by alerting you that something is wrong.

As women, we own our bodies. No one else is entitled to control your body—only you, because it's yours. Respect… Your body doesn't lie, even when your mind may overthink the situation. In fact, your mind can talk you out of what your body already experiences and intuitively knows. Your body knows that, for whatever reason, you are not where you are supposed to be, you are not doing what you are supposed to be doing.

Your body can also let you know when things are great. It can tell you when you are with wonderful company and experiencing bliss. Vibrating with excitement or trembling in fear are ways your body speaks to you. Are you paying attention?

Affirmation

I am aware of what I am feeling in my body and how it responds to what is going on around me.

Holistic Prescription

 Call to Action

Take notes and notice how your body speaks to you when you are stressed.

 Mother Nature

Use these herbs: allspice for self-awareness, emotional healing, and luck; lemon balm for physical restoration; and bay leaves for spiritual enhancement and protection.

 Gemstones

Activate these gemstones: bloodstone for physical strength; amethyst for fortification and spiritual awareness; and hematite for physical healing.

 Feng Shui

For optimal feng shui balance and harmony: Clear all clutter; add wood elements like plants and flowers, plus earth colors yellow and orange for self-care, inspiration, and vitality; add white, pink, and red candles of the fire element for awareness, self-love, and energy.

2

LISTEN TO YOUR PHYSICAL SELF

Your body speaks to you all the time. You might often ignore it. But it is critical that you listen to what it is telling you.

Respectful communication begins within yourself, along with careful attention to what your body is telling you. When your physical self starts to talk, try not to mind-talk your way out of feeling what you feel. If your body senses danger, listen and believe it!

Identity paralysis occurs when your mind, body, and spirit get stuck in an endless loop of resistance and confusion about change, which is stressful. Are you also stuck in a reactive cycle of lather, rinse, and repeat when it comes to disease? That is a situation that medical professionals call *chronic*.

Being in a constant state of fight or flight can cause real harm to your body. Some examples are stomach pain and digestive issues, headaches including migraines, and heart palpitations with high blood pressure, in addition to self-destructive behaviors in an attempt to soothe yourself, like irresponsible shopping, drinking, smoking, eating, sexing, and drugging.

Yes, stress throws everything off-balance. Change can create this stress, but so can unresolved trauma, emotional conflicts, and anger. These can fester and create physical symptoms too.

When we are in tune with our bodies, we can sense that something is wrong well ahead of a medical diagnosis, medication, or surgery, even before we experience a physical illness. It is the best way to check for and stay in balance.

Affirmation

I love my body and appreciate everything it does for me.

Holistic Prescription

 Call to Action

Unplug and, in silence, feel what your body is telling you.

 Mother Nature

Use these herbs and flowers: lavender for peaceful relaxation and restorative rest; rosemary for purified physical healing love; and gardenia for expansive healing and peaceful self-love.

 Gemstones

Activate these gemstones: smoky quartz for grounding and balance; turquoise for health and inner calm; and garnet for chi stimulation and to remove emotional blockages in the body.

 Feng Shui

For optimal feng shui balance and harmony: Clear clutter from your environment to also clear your mind and body; use earth elements such as the colors yellow and brown, plus natural fabrics and textures for health, self-care, and stability; use wood elements such as plants to purify the air, flowers to bring in more yin, and the color green for vitality and healing.

3

REDUCE BODY DISTRESS

Most of us are judged by the way we look—especially women. It's so unfair! Your appearance is not who you are. It seems obvious that you are not what your physical self looks like, yet so many stereotypes, labels, and assumptions are related to our bodies. Of course, there is so much more to who and what we are. When we reclaim our bodies, we reclaim our identities. We reclaim ourselves.

Self-acceptance is the key to self-love and self-esteem. I love my body, and I hope that you do too. Let's go even deeper. Caring for ourselves by reducing body distress is an act of self-love.

When it comes to health, it is not the appearance of our bodies that matters most, but the condition of our bodies. Sometimes this truth can be seen and felt physically, but most times it cannot. When you reclaim your body, you may be tempted to ask, "How does my body look?" Instead, I encourage you to ask yourself, "How does my body feel?" Many of us may be shocked to realize that our bodies are actually in distress.

If you knew how simple it was to reduce distress in your body, I bet you would do it all the time. I hope you will. What do you need to do? You need to relax. You are learning how to do it right now.

As women, we are often expected to be caretakers of the world. Three words: quality of life! Relaxation allows us to process life and derive benefit from it. This is the best way to live. By doing so, we create a new paradigm for what is acceptable, what is preferred, and what is "normal."

We can create a new reality that includes and even prioritizes our emotional well-being as critical to our physical health. Because it is. Our bodies need it so badly! We can do this individually and collectively by maximizing the potential of relaxation.

Let go. Let your body be what it is. The key to relaxation and letting go is knowing that you can. Do it anytime. Any place. This is your moment to…relax. Let it go.

Affirmation

> *I release all worries, distress, and frustrations, watching them drift up and away, out of my body, into droplets that disperse and disappear into the Universe.*

Holistic Prescription

 Call to Action
Increase self-awareness by doing a daily body check-in to see how you feel.

 Mother Nature
Use these herbs: green tea for physical body regulation; sage for spiritual purification and new positive beginnings; and juniper berries for releasing negativity.

 Gemstones
Activate these gemstones: bloodstone for strengthening the body; selenite for dispelling negative energy; and jade for wisdom, peace, heart energy, and harmony.

 Feng Shui
For optimal feng shui balance and harmony: Use earth colors yellow, orange, and tan to ground yourself; add more earth elements like potted plants for self-care and boundaries.

4

RELAX TO HEAL

Many of us are taking care of other people. So much so that we get used to putting them first. Who is taking care of you? You are important too! It's time to take care of yourself.

I know it probably feels different when you make yourself a priority. Maybe you don't quite understand that this is exactly what healthy people do. Healthy people know when and how to take care of themselves. Healthy people rest and relax on a regular basis.

Healing is possible when you dare to explore the lengths and depths of relaxation. If you look deep into your heart, it is there, waiting for you to acknowledge this need and say, "Yes, I will."

For most people, their healing journey includes meditation, yoga, and deep breathing, all things that help their minds, bodies, and spirits to settle down. When we perform these activities consistently on a daily basis, they are helpful. For you, relaxation may look a little different, and that's okay too.

Sometimes, relaxing to heal doesn't look like anything at all. Other times, it's a painful process with difficult lessons and challenging people: Crying, struggling, and working through it the best way we know how.

Relaxation is how we heal. If we don't relax, we don't heal.

We all need to relax and let go because change is a constant. With change, our balance is disrupted and peace is upended. Use relaxation and letting go to resettle into a fresh, updated, peaceful equilibrium, back into your natural state of harmonious being.

Yes, you can relax. Yes, you can heal. Yes, you can reconnect to your inner being of balance, calmness, clarity, and peace. And for you, maybe this means revisiting the past to release old ideas and notions to make space for new beliefs and a new vision of how life can be. Maybe it means conquering your fear of what may or may not be real or easy.

Relax you will. And heal you shall.

Your relaxation healing journey starts with a simple realization, then a single step, and another, and another. I know you see it. Now, it's time to live it. Let's go.

Affirmation

> *Every day, I relax my mind, body, and spirit, allowing my healing energy to work its magic.*

Holistic Prescription

Call to Action

Identify a special location where you can go to relax and heal every day.

Mother Nature

Use these herbs: sage for cleansing and purification; juniper berries for releasing negativity; and chamomile for relaxation.

Gemstones

Activate these gemstones: labradorite for intuition and to protect your aura; howlite for remaining true to yourself and to soothe emotions; and aventurine to bring joy, acceptance, and well-being.

Feng Shui

For optimal feng shui balance and harmony: Use earth colors like tan for grounding; add green, blue, and teal to promote relaxation and calm; add wood elements like furniture and plants to promote healing; add water elements like circles and blue colors for relaxation and letting go.

5

INVEST IN YOURSELF

How do you make a decision? Who do you consider to be most important in this process? What are your values and priorities? I encourage you to start putting yourself first. This means considering what works best for you when you do what you do, every day.

Many of us don't think twice about saving money in a bank, maintaining a retirement fund, or buying stocks. That's great, because planning for the future and being prepared are important. But let me ask you this: What did you do to invest in yourself today?

When you are well, your family and loved ones are well too. This is true of all types of wealth in your life, including finances, health and wellness, and fun.

I am not talking about the narcissist. I am talking to women who grew up learning that sacrificing for others is normal and expected. We all know women who invest in their significant others, children, work, family, and friends yet fail to put the same time, energy, and resources into themselves. Who taught you that putting yourself last is acceptable, as long as others are satisfied in the process? Those outdated concepts keep you trapped.

If we keep going this way, peace, joy, and healthy relationships are elusive and our health suffers. Why? We can't be everything to everybody if we are not being what we need for ourselves.

Some of us have neglected ourselves so much that we do not know what investing in ourselves looks like. Time to refresh! You invest in yourself when you:

- Surround yourself with positive people.
- Do something fun or relaxing.
- Maintain high ethical standards.

Sometimes you have to be reminded that you are your most valuable asset. Our most valuable assets are protected. Just like the oxygen mask on the airplane, you have to put yourself first. Don't forget to invest in yourself today.

Affirmation

I am my own best thing and most valuable asset, deserving all of my love, time, and attention.

Holistic Prescription

 Call to Action
Schedule "me" time in your calendar at the beginning of every day.

 Mother Nature
Use these plants: rose for increasing love vibrations, including self-love; honeysuckle for beauty, personal power, and self-love; and lime to promote healing that prioritizes love.

 Gemstones
Activate these gemstones: pyrite for transformative healing; carnelian for strength, self-worth, and confidence; and lapis for wisdom and serene awareness.

 Feng Shui
For optimal feng shui balance and harmony: Add white, gray, and gold/silver/copper metallic colors for joy and beauty; use wood elements like plants and flowers for self-care and boundaries, green and blue colors for vitality, and fire elements like candles for confidence and inspiration.

6

LISTEN AND ACT

Before seeking higher educational goals, living on our own, having children, experiencing multiple hurts and betrayals, we were much better at doing what was in our best interests. When we were hungry, we ate. When we were tired, we slept. When we were sad, we cried. When we were happy, we laughed.

Today, many of us have difficulties coping with pain, stress, and disappointment. Sometimes we get overwhelmed. It may feel like we are treading water in an endless sea.

When it's time to rest, rest.

Many of us have been taught to ignore our intuitive need to chill out. More productive in the short term, burned out in the end. To enjoy life to the fullest, we need moments of chill.

You can gravitate naturally to relaxation when you respond to your own basic instincts. That's your intuition. When you hear and honor intuition, you are living in harmony with the Universe. Listen to it and act. To chill is natural. Do you honor yourself in this way? Do you realize that you can let fear and anxiety fade away?

People who worry and stress out regularly are more likely to experience health issues, including rapid cognitive decline, as they age. And they rarely bounce back. Please don't be a woman who burns herself into the ground. You can do better.

When you listen and respond to your need to chill out, you do not need to justify yourself to anyone.

Affirmation

I honor my need to chill out by listening and acting in the
best interest of my mind, body, and spirit.

Holistic Prescription

 Call to Action

When someone asks you "Why are you chilling out?" Tell
them "It's what I was told to do."

 Mother Nature

Use these herbs: skullcap for releasing and relinquishing control; cedarwood for positive new beginnings; and chamomile
for calming relaxation.

 Gemstones

Activate these gemstones: tiger's eye for increasing confidence
while releasing fear and anxiety; moss agate for increased
immune functioning, happiness, and overall balance; and
aquamarine to clear the mind and connect to higher health
and well-being.

 Feng Shui

For optimal feng shui balance and harmony: Add metal colors, such as white and gray, plus metal furnishing accents for
clarity and integrity; add wood elements with plants, such as
cedar, honeysuckle, peony, hibiscus, lime, and orchid; add the
color red, such as red pillows and candles, for confidence and
positive, dynamic energy.

7

SHOW AND PROVE: "I LOVE ME"

How you show up for others is not nearly as important as how you show up for yourself. How did you show up for yourself today?

"I love me."

It's a declaration that is basic, yet full of passion. Childlike in its purity, yet timeless, this proclamation is for all ages. And it just might be the right thing for you at this time in your life.

"I love me."

You are your own best thing. Professing love to yourself for yourself just makes sense. Yet it is one of the most difficult philosophies for us to fully accept, embrace, and live by.

"I love me."

What other people say about you is not nearly as important as what you say to yourself.

"I love me."

It is the foundation of your relationship with yourself. Everything you do and say can come from this foundational reality if you choose it to be so.

"I love me."

Who you think you are may change as you grow. Your identity will evolve. Still…

"I love me."

Always and forever. Now, prove it.

Affirmation

I love myself today and every day: I love me.

Holistic Prescription

 Call to Action

Remind yourself that you are magical, special, and honorable in the most unexpected ways.

 Mother Nature

Use these herbs: rosemary for pure, healing love; cinnamon for grounding and balancing energy; and yarrow for protecting and raising the frequency of love vibrations.

 Gemstones

Activate these gemstones: rose quartz for warm, caring, gentle self-love and emotional healing by releasing resentments; moonstone for self-protection and good fortune; and aventurine for nurturing yourself, bringing joy, and a positive attitude.

 Feng Shui

For optimal feng shui balance and harmony: Surround yourself with love and beauty, such as gorgeous artwork, mirrors, candles, plants, and flowers; clear all clutter in your home; bring more feminine (yin) elements into your work space and home, especially your bedroom—for example, curvy furniture, soft textures, and pastel colors like pink and yellow; add metal for joy and beauty; add wood for growth and healing; add red (fire element) for love, passion, and inspiration.

8

REACTIVATE YOUR HEART

One heart, one love. When your heart energy is activated, it extends across the Universe. Love is the ultimate connector, unifying us all. A hug is transformative.

Care + passion = love energy.

But sometimes love hurts us, and we are in pain. It is our nature to love and be loved. After heartbreak, we tend to close ourselves off to love and affection. Not only are we closing the door to pain, but we are also closing the door to what we need at a time when we need it the most. When our love energy is low and depleted, we feel it!

In the world, there is light and dark. Pain and pleasure. Good and bad. Instead of thinking in terms of black and white, yes or no, let's look at the shades of gray in-between. There is hope here. And optimism can win the day *and* bring back your heart energy.

You live a heart-filled life by giving love, of course, but also by receiving it. You can love the one you're with and still keep your heart open for more.

If you've had a hard time in love, don't despair. Love is there for everyone. Reactivate your heart with the natural first step: self-love. If you don't fully love yourself, how can you expect others to love you?

Learning to be at one with your heart can transform your entire life. Helping you love yourself...it also attracts more love from others.

Place your hand on your heart and declare unconditional love for yourself. Then, write down the people, places, animals, foods, and anything else that you are passionate about. And don't underestimate the power of the cuddle! Nice touching is good, as are the erotic and the compassionate.

As you live your life, be careful not to give all of your love away. Keep some for yourself.

Affirmation

I am love.

Holistic Prescription

 Call to Action
Think loving thoughts, read loving books, and watch loving movies.

 Mother Nature
Use these herbs and flowers: honeysuckle for personal power and increased feminine power; rose for increasing self-love energy; and cinnamon for grounding and balance.

 Gemstones
Activate these gemstones: rose quartz for warm, caring, gentle self-love and emotional healing by releasing resentments; malachite for purification and attracting love by opening the heart; and lepidolite for attracting love, hope, and light, plus change acceptance.

 Feng Shui
For optimal feng shui balance and harmony: Add circular metal furnishings (water and metal elements) for joy, beauty, and connection; add pink and red flowers and plants (fire and wood elements) for self-love, love, and passion; add pairs of items in the bedroom for romance.

9

TAKE BACK YOUR ENERGY

Feeling tired lately? Where is your energy? You can reclaim your emotional, physical, and mental vitality. Call it back to you *now*.

Technology can be demanding. People too. You've got an obligation to optimize your health. You have the right to disconnect and make yourself less available. Women in business often feel the pressure to reply to an email *immediately*, respond to a customer inquiry *immediately*, produce a requested document *immediately*.

Empowered women have no masters.

Like a cat meowing for attention, a significant other expecting a homemade dinner, a voicemail waiting to be played, we tend to respond as if everything is an emergency. Even when it's not.

It all just seems so important at the time. But…a demand is actually a request. An expectation. Not a requirement. The pressure to always be available is the pressure we impose on ourselves. We are taught to be oh so compliant and fully responsive. What if we just ignored these calls?

You have the right to exercise your options, to wait and create space to respond to non-emergencies in your own time. What will happen when you do? Probably nothing. They'll adjust.

Have you been spoiling people? Probably. Is it under your control to make it better? Absolutely. We can be loving and responsive, just not always immediately for everyone all the time. Why not? Because a sense of urgency is created where there is none. We get stressed out for no good reason, for all issues both large and small.

That "right now" energy they want from you is the same energy that you need for yourself. So, take it back and stop giving it away so easily. Stay vigilant and self-aware to resist their demands.

Do you live for you, or do you exist to be utilized by other people? You may find that when you step back and do less, you give the people around you a chance to step up into who and what *they* are. By saying "no," you are reclaiming your time, your energy, and your self, plus helping other people do what they are supposed to do.

Affirmation

Holistic Prescription

Call to Action

Establish time periods for your availability. Be consistent with your time when you are available and when you are not.

Mother Nature

Use these herbs: cayenne for physical stimulation; ginger for getting rid of something old and replacing it with something new and better; and thyme for spiritual awareness, plus healing with love and courage.

Gemstones

Activate these gemstones: sodalite for getting in tune with your intuition and higher consciousness; petrified wood for purification and grounding; onyx for emotional and physical strength; and moss agate for increased immune functioning, happiness, and overall balance.

Feng Shui

For optimal feng shui balance and harmony: Opt for high ceilings and tall chairs to sit straight with good posture; be a woman in charge and sit at the head of a long, narrow wooden table; use floor seating like pillows, cushions, and low stools to stay grounded.

10

PROTECT YOUR HEART

When you expect others to treat you the way that you treat them and they don't, it hurts. When a long-term relationship ends, it can feel like being stabbed in the heart. Even if the other person was being selfish, emotionally unavailable, or immature, it is not surprising that you would feel brokenhearted and betrayed, at least at first. It can be a brutal lesson to learn. Maybe you gave this undeserving person too much of yourself. Did you give away your most special and unique loving energy? We all have been there. Now, you have the tools to take your love back.

In entry 9: Take Back Your Energy, you learned how to reclaim your energy. Love is energy too. It's the best kind. When you love yourself completely, you prioritize self-care (easily!), but did you know that a key part of self-care is protecting your heart?

Your heart is sacred. How would you describe this space? What does it feel like to give and receive from here? Does this space have a color? A physical sensation?

The *anahata* or heart chakra is the fourth chakra, according to Hindu Yogic, Shakta, and Buddhist Tantric traditions. In Sanskrit, *anahata* means "unhurt, unstruck, and unbeaten." The heart chakra is associated with love, balance, calmness, serenity, compassion, and forgiveness. When it is in a weakened or unbalanced state, we fail to give love fully and completely, and we are unable to fully and completely accept love, including self-love.

You and only you can activate your *anahata* to heal and protect this sacred space from being violated.

Even if you gave all of your love away, you can take it back. Why stop there? Going further, apply that love that you retrieved to yourself and, now (lesson fully learned), guard your sacred heart space.

You can protect your heart, not with a barbed wire barrier but with a ring of white, pink, and yellow light that you visualize in your mind's eye. After working on this visualization technique for a while, your protection will become an aura so bright, strong, and beautiful that only the truly worthy would even dare try to enter it.

Affirmation

> **I protect my heart with a beautiful aura that only goodness and positivity can enter.**

Holistic Prescription

 Call to Action

Visualize what guarding your sacred heart space looks like: big, beautiful, and bright.

 Mother Nature

Use these herbs and flowers: rose for increasing love vibrations, including self-love; cinnamon for grounding and balancing energy; and yarrow for raising the frequency of love vibrations.

 Gemstones:

Activate these gemstones: rhodonite for stimulating, clearing, and activating the heart; chrysoprase to help you recognize the grace and beauty in yourself; and apatite for willpower and strength through love.

 Feng Shui

For optimal feng shui balance and harmony: Use white, yellow, pink, and magenta colors to promote calming love and heal the heart; use water elements like round shapes to stay connected; use earth colors yellow and orange for self-care and boundaries; use red candles for passionate love.

11

DISCOVER NATURAL HEALING

Natural healing is the best form of therapy. Nature helps you heal and realize that you are never alone in the world. A natural environment helps you feel your feelings rather than repress them. Women who like animals are also in tune with nature.

Tuning into nature is healthy. Don't just take my word for it; studies show that people influenced by nature tend to be more grounded, calm, generous, and even intelligent! And there's more: Healing through nature is a scientific fact. Embracing nature is like a vaccine for prevention and like an antibiotic to treat an infection. Yes, it's true. Nature is both the prevention and the cure.

Nature therapy is more than a thing; it is *the* thing you need for chilling out. Using nature to heal, maintain your health, and be well…it sounds so intuitive. Because it is.

Nature is the epitome of feminine power. In nature, you can be free! Don't hesitate to surround yourself with Her glory. Put plants in your room. Observe them, feel the leaves, smell them, and consciously acknowledge that they are there by complimenting them on their shapes, colors, and textures. Better yet, go outside and look at the sky. Breathe deeply, in and out several times. Touch your toes. Do some twists. Stretch your body, hold your hands to the sky, then plant your feet firmly in the ground. Feel the difference this special moment creates. It feels so good, and the best thing is: You can do it every day, whenever you want.

When you are in nature, focus on the sounds and smells, and feel the pulse of it everywhere and in everything. We are part of nature, and like us, the rest of the world is alive too. Stop ignoring it and feel it. You need it, just like water and food. And your health, especially your mental health, will thank you.

Affirmation

Holistic Prescription

 Call to Action

When you find yourself sitting for long periods of time, get out and go for a walk, even if it is just around the block. Notice nature: all the sights, scents, and sounds.

 Mother Nature

Use these herbs: parsley for detoxification; black cohosh for hormone regulation; and echinacea and elderberry to increase immune function.

 Gemstones

Activate these gemstones: black tourmaline for higher elevated thinking; jade for wisdom, peace, heart energy, and harmony; and amethyst for fortification and spiritual awareness.

 Feng Shui

For optimal feng shui balance and harmony: Include all five elements (water, wood, earth, metal, fire) for natural balance; use metal and wood furniture, a water fountain or water colors, and purifying plants; hang artwork featuring green spaces, trees, flowers, the ocean, lakes, rivers, and other beautiful nature scenes.

12

USE YOUR NOSE

Smell. Sight. Hearing. Touch. Taste. We have way more than five senses, but this is a good, basic start to increase self-awareness and help us achieve balance. One of our most underutilized senses is our sense of smell.

Have you ever walked into a room and smelled something really bad? Just the thought of certain smells can make me feel physically ill and put a scowl on my face. On the other hand, have you ever walked into a room and smelled something so wonderful that you *had* to know what it was? Nice, right?

Whether we realize it or not, we are constantly smelling, all the time. The real question is: What do you prefer to smell right now? Let's make sure we are smelling positive and uplifting things so that we can be positively uplifted.

When we are more aware of how smells affect how we feel, we can exploit this powerful connection for our benefit.

I recommend getting sensual with scents! The positive impacts of aromatherapy and herbs should not be underestimated. Natural smells are not just nice; they are scientifically proven to elevate your mood to make you feel better. And *that* is a powerful thing.

Our sense of smell is always at work, which means it is always affecting us. Let's be intentional and use it to help us. For example, the scent of lavender helps you relax and enhances sleep. The smell of roses makes you feel loving and beautiful. Smelling chocolate chip cookies might remind you of the comforts of home.

Don't stop with just smell. We can also explore our other senses more fully to experience a more complete human existence! It's sensual and fun, so good and necessary right now.

Affirmation

I feel and experience my life as a sensual being, surrounding myself with things that make me feel whole, full of love, and beautiful.

Holistic Prescription

 Call to Action

Choose a candle with a great scent and light it at your desk or in your bedroom. Note what you like about it. Enjoy the smell by inhaling deeply.

 Mother Nature

Use these herbs and flowers: allspice for self-awareness, emotional healing, and luck; honeysuckle for beauty, personal power, and self-love; and jasmine for self-worth, beauty, and spiritual awareness.

 Gemstones

Activate these gemstones: turquoise for general health and inner calm; black tourmaline for higher elevated thinking; and moss agate for increased immune functioning, happiness, and overall balance.

 Feng Shui

For optimal feng shui balance and harmony: Add fire to your space by using a scented candle to meditate, manifest, or empty your mind of busy chi with a candle meditation; use pairs of candles if you want to start or improve your relationship; use metal accents to add joy and beauty.

13

USE FLOWER POWER

Among the beautiful treasures Mother Nature offers us, flowers are a favorite. Don't you just love the smell of fresh blooms? Women who surround themselves with flowers are women who prioritize beauty and healing. There is strong evidence that all plants, including flowers, have astounding abilities to sense and react to the world around them, that they remember, and even react, in ways similar to humans. In many ways, flowers are our friends.

More than looking pretty and smelling wonderful, flowering plants help us chill out and be heathier. For example, lavender and jasmine have proven sleep-enhancing and sleep-inducing properties that promote relaxation and biophysical restoration. And that's only two flowering plants out of millions!

Flowers are just one of nature's many gifts to humans. Science also confirms that, like the smell of salty ocean air or a pine forest or freshly cut grass, the smell of flowers is linked to greater retention of information, enhanced mood, and emotional well-being.

Although science can provide some basics about the mechanisms behind aromatherapy, ultimately it doesn't have all of the answers. And that's okay. As helpful as it is, science does not begin to explain why you instinctively and intuitively enjoy the specific types of plants and flowers that you do. The fact that they make you feel good is what counts. And, yes, it is enough.

We do not need to know why we love the smell of something to know that we like how it makes us feel. If having a particular plant or flower around you brings you joy, get it. Grow it. Love it. Keep it. Treasure the moments it creates.

Put simply, when you smell pretty flowers, it makes you feel good. Your brain, in turn, releases more positive signals back to you. The result is a happier and more balanced, relaxed, and positive state. The fact that a flower can do that is amazing. Who knew?

Affirmation

Like a flower, I am blossoming.

Holistic Prescription

 Call to Action

Choose potted flowers like orchids and bulbs to place in your home instead of cut flowers because they live longer and produce more when they are whole and uncut.

 Mother Nature

Use these herbs and flowers: peony for calm brightening; gardenia for expansive healing and peaceful self-love; and lavender for peaceful relaxation and restorative rest.

 Gemstones

Activate these gemstones: amethyst for fortification and spiritual awareness; blue agate for patience, peace, hope, and positive thinking; and fluorite for peace and increasing mental clarity.

 Feng Shui

For optimal feng shui balance and harmony: Grow flowers in your backyard or patio garden; put cut flowers in bowls or vases throughout your home to increase positive yin (feminine) energy.

14

SET YOURSELF FREE
WITH MOTHER NATURE

Nature fulfills us by being Herself. Imagine the feeling that you get when you climb a mountain peak, inhale the ocean air, run your fingers through the water in a river stream, or feel the sun on your face. It feels like if you ceased to exist right now, it would be all right. But you're not finished yet….Don't cease to exist—live! Live freely. Live and spread the joy. Feel the tangible health benefits of indelible sensations. Feel Mother Nature and all that She has to offer. Your life and Hers are interconnected.

If you look at newborn babies and the way that they grow through childhood, they simultaneously observe the world, learn, adapt, and relax. This is exactly what we must do every day to grow and self-actualize. Because it is a natural process. Mother Nature is there to help us. She wants us to grow and be free, just like Her. No matter what goes on in our hectic and sometimes confusing and contrary lives, our universal mother, Mother Nature, is always there for us. Every morning when we wake up, She's there, without fail.

We can connect with all types of life when we immerse ourselves in a more natural environment like being around oceans, rivers, trees, and mountains. When your holistic health lifestyle includes intentional exposure to Mother Nature every day, you *will* thrive. Now, is that enough motivation to create a more sustainable lifestyle?

Let's make it a priority.

Affirmation

> Today, I feel the trees, the water, and the earth to connect with nature's healing power, infinite glory, and potential.

Holistic Prescription

 Call to Action

Fill your work and personal spaces with plants, flowers, and greenery.

 Mother Nature

Use these herbs: sage for spiritual purification and new positive beginnings; chamomile for calming relaxation; and rosemary for purified physical healing love.

 Gemstones

Activate these gemstones: jade for wisdom, peace, heart energy, and harmony; aquamarine to clear the mind and connect to higher health and well-being; and aventurine to bring joy, acceptance, and well-being.

 Feng Shui

For optimal feng shui balance and harmony: Include equal elements of water, wood, earth, metal, and fire in your home to heal; use cedarwood, candles, plants, and flowers; include circular white and metal furnishings and the colors of the ocean, such as blue and turquoise; use nature-inspired artwork on your walls and soft, natural fabrics.

15

ABSORB JOY AND GRATITUDE

Have you ever gone to a beautiful, exotic locale only to get food poisoning? Maybe your body tensed up, your face tightened, and you were sick and miserable to be around. Later, when you healed and felt better, how did you recall the trip?

Did you focus on how blessed you were to be on that trip and on the days that were awesome where you felt happy? Or do you cringe and remember how terrible the food poisoning experience was? The way your mind works…you can make a choice: to smile and remember this trip fondly as one of the best experiences in your life, or frown and concentrate on the bad thing that happened.

When we choose joy, we focus on the good parts of our experiences, which are plentiful, instead of the pain experienced when things did not go our way. By absorbing joy, we set ourselves up for smiling. Did you know joy is a life skill? And smiling is contagious.

We all have good stuff going on in our lives. And sometimes we hit a rough patch in our journey. By focusing on the good things, identifying positivity in our everyday lives, we can feel better more often, thus absorbing joy. There is wonder everywhere, which means joy is everywhere too!

Don't just feel joy, absorb it. Take it *all in*. And add gratitude. Expressing gratitude is useful if you are experiencing blockages in moving forward, especially if you are in a state of emotional distress. We can all benefit from strategies that help us focus on the more fun aspects of our lives. It's not always doom and gloom all the time, and our hardest times are temporary. This philosophy provides the clarity and balance required for a healthy lifestyle.

Rest creates space for joy. By keeping your well of joy and gratitude full, you can keep anxiety and depression further away, moving quickly through any challenges that come your way. Health and relaxation are waiting for you.

Affirmation

I am grateful for the wonderful things in my life; joy radiates within me.

Holistic Prescription

 Call to Action

Make a habit of taking in good feelings fully and completely. Practice letting go of the past.

 Mother Nature

Use these herbs and flowers: basil to reduce anxiety, sad feelings, and stress; rosemary for purified physical healing love; and passionflower to reduce restlessness, anxiety, and insomnia.

 Gemstones

Activate these gemstones: citrine for enhanced manifestation, personal will, and prosperity; alexandrite for identifying and developing joy within yourself; peridot for positive energy, sunshine, and abundant blessings; and moss agate for increased immune functioning, happiness, and overall balance.

 Feng Shui

For optimal feng shui balance and harmony: Make sure your home includes plenty of sunlight to bring in positivity; bring in the outdoors with plants and the color green; open the windows regularly for clean, fresh air; bring in a water fountain for soothing nature-inspired sounds; use metal elements like mirrors to bring in joy and beauty.

16

FEEL YOUR FEELINGS

Sometimes, you just gotta feel. Get in touch with who you are and how you are. Allowing yourself to feel your emotions is being honest, present, and brave. In the moment. Feel your feelings fully and completely, if and when you must. Scream. Cry. Laugh. Yell. Pound a pillow. Collapse on the floor. Jump up and down. Kiss your dog. Lie in the fetal position. Dance naked.

Honor your feelings. Trust them. And when you've finished, quickly let them go! Then, you can move on with your life. Without fear. No regret. No shame.

Your feelings are good and healthy and valid and important. However, they are also fleeting.

You can feel ten different ways in ten minutes and overanalyze a thousand times in your head why you feel the way that you feel when really it is so much more basic than that. Feel what you feel when you feel it 100 percent so that you are fully in touch with your emotions and able to let them go to move onto the next.

You are not your feelings. A brief moment when you were happy, sad, disappointed, angry, or upset does not define you. Remarkable and complex, good or bad, a simple emotion is just a snapshot in time.

No matter how sensitive you are, your soul's capacity is so much greater than just a few feelings.

Affirmation

Holistic Prescription

Call to Action

Pay special attention to how you feel and stop acting like you're feeling fine when you're not.

Mother Nature

Use these herbs: bay leaves for protection; cinnamon for grounding and balancing energy; juniper berries for releasing negativity.

Gemstones

Activate these gemstones: tiger's eye for increasing confidence while releasing fear and anxiety; aventurine to bring joy, acceptance, and well-being; and pyrite for transformative healing.

Feng Shui

For optimal feng shui balance and harmony: Clear all clutter; use the color teal for deep wisdom and connection (water element); use earth elements like square shapes and ceramic vases for grounding and stability; add sunshine and metal furnishings (fire and metal elements) for joy.

17

GET RESTORATIVE REST

Is "doing nothing" better than "doing something"? You betcha. Lots of things look like doing nothing but are actually doing something great for yourself. For example:

- Healing
- Deliberating
- Contemplating
- Visioning
- Planning

- Strategizing
- Absorbing
- Dreaming
- Manifesting
- Replenishing

- Recuperating
- Loving
- Leading
- Being
- Elevating

Clearly, these are productive actions. Taking the time, even if you must schedule these blocks in your day, means that you prioritize getting restorative rest, the epitome of self-care.

Rest is a counterbalance to stress and anxiety. We have been taught that lack of activity is equated with lack of valuable contribution. Nope, not true! On the contrary, rest adds value to your life. Only when you rest can you become restored and renewed. Energy in, energy out, rest. Simple.

The ultimate rest is sleep. Are you getting enough deep sleep? We hear a lot about diet and exercise, but not so much about sleep. The three coexist together and are equal in importance. You optimize your health when you prioritize all three, not one over the other. All are necessary to maintain our physical, mental, and spiritual health. Midday naps have been shown to increase immune system functioning and other indicators of health. Taken once or twice a week, naps have also been shown to reduce the risk of major cardiovascular health emergencies, including heart attack and stroke, by almost half.

Are you convinced? Take time to rest.

Affirmation

> *I maintain my productivity and energy levels by taking restful breaks and getting deep sleep.*

Holistic Prescription

 Call to Action

Ignore the naysayers who claim you are "doing nothing." You are not obligated to explain your unique health and healing process to anyone.

 Mother Nature

Use these herbs: lavender for peaceful relaxation and restorative rest; chamomile for calming relaxation; and passionflower for reducing restlessness, anxiety, and insomnia.

 Gemstones

Activate these gemstones: turquoise for health and inner calm; blue agate for patience, peace, hope, and positive thinking; and larimar for stillness, calm, and chilling vibes.

 Feng Shui

For optimal feng shui balance and harmony: Use an established headboard for stability and place your bed with the head facing south; clear all clutter from under your bed; reduce the use of electronics in your bedroom; use soft and comfortable bedding; add wood elements like plants and earth elements like yellow and beige colors for grounding, self-care, and boundaries; add yin (feminine) soft textures.

18

ADD COMMON SCENTS

It is fairly easy to create herbal formulas for your daily benefit. The most beneficial herbs are not usually exotic, expensive, or hard to find. In fact, you may have them in your kitchen. Here are some ways you can incorporate herbs into your lifestyle:

- Burn the herb on a charcoal block or in a fireproof resin incense burner.
- Bathe with it. Be sure to use a gauze or tea bag to prevent clogs in your plumbing.
- Drink it as a tea (hot or cold). Always make sure the herb is edible and safe for consumption.
- Make it into a body oil. Soak and strain herbs in jojoba, almond, vitamin E, olive, shea, or coconut oil, individually or blended.

An easy and great herbal remedy is to create an herbal spray. First choose an herb that you like. Then take an empty spritzer bottle and fill it with your chosen herb (or its essential oil) along with distilled water to create an herbal mist. (If you are using whole herbs, you may want to strain them out to prevent the nozzle from clogging.)

You can spray your herbal mist on your linens and your clothes, in your car, around your bedroom, throughout your work area, and anywhere you would like to experience the scent. After a few days, do you notice a difference? You should be able to feel a gentle shift in your mood.

In this way, common scents help you have common sense.

In addition to herbs, other natural elements have been shown to be helpful for relaxation and letting go, namely, salt (especially sea salt) and vanilla. You can use these ingredients in your baths and on food, or create a misting spray with distilled water. Of course, eating them is fun too!

As you get more familiar with the herbal remedy process, you can also venture into making soaps, herbal washes, and herb butters.

Affirmation

I use the natural elements around me to uplift me and soothe my soul.

Holistic Prescription

 Call to Action

Use herbal mixtures as a secret weapon to help you achieve peace and balance.

 Mother Nature

Use these herbs and flowers: thyme for spiritual awareness, plus healing with love and courage; clove for physical stimulation and positive energy attraction; and honeysuckle for beauty, personal power, and self-love.

 Gemstones

Activate these gemstones: labradorite for intuition and to protect your aura; jade for wisdom, peace, heart energy, and harmony; and clear quartz for purification and inspiring creativity.

 Feng Shui

For optimal feng shui balance and harmony: Clear clutter in your kitchen and maintain a balance of the five elements (water, wood, earth, metal, fire); in your kitchen, use healing colors yellow, orange, and brown.

19

REGULATE NATURALLY

Is your spirit consistently attracted to herbology and the medicinal uses of herbs and natural plants? It's fun and fascinating! Herbs are part of nature and can also be part of your self-expression when you create, wear, cook, or bathe with them. There are many herbs that are healing, offer spiritual protection, and, yes, help you relax and let go. The focus here, specifically, is balance. Some of these herbs may be in your kitchen while others are less common.

Herbs are potent plants that should be treated with the utmost respect and care. Like all medicines, they should be used with caution as they can interact with other medications you may use. Unlike drugs that are chemically altered and manufactured in a lab, herbs grow in nature and are holistic, influencing your entire being. They are also readily accessible for most people, and you can grow many types of herbs in your backyard, patio, or kitchen windowsill. Although each herb has unique properties and may influence each person differently, there are some that have been proven to be more beneficial than others, especially for peace and calm.

Some simple herbal remedies include the following:

- Drink herbal tea using a homemade or store-bought blend of your favorite herbs, including herbs good for cleansing, detoxification, digestion, and elimination, such as turmeric, milk thistle, cilantro, basil, fennel seed, licorice, dandelion root, senna, cascara, and yellow dock.
- Grow herbal plants and use in your cooking, including cilantro, peppermint, basil, thyme, rosemary, lavender, and allspice.
- Burn herbs on charcoal blocks in a fireproof container. Herbs good for this application include sage, bay leaves, cedarwood, pine, peppermint, spearmint, juniper berries, and cinnamon.
- Create an herbal linen spray for your bed using 8 ounces of distilled water, a couple of tablespoons of lemon (leaves,

zest, or juice), a pinch of sea salt, a cup of the petals or about twenty drops of essential oil from a sweet-smelling flower like rose, gardenia, honeysuckle, or peony.

Affirmation

I am naturally drawn to herbs that will balance and heal me to help me be my highest self.

Holistic Prescription

Call to Action

Maintain a supply of go-to herbs when you are in need—for example, herbs that help you relax and find peace when you've had an eventful day.

Mother Nature

Use these herbs: cedarwood for positive new beginnings; skullcap for releasing and relinquishing control; and black cohosh for hormone regulation.

Gemstones

Activate these gemstones: petrified wood for purification and grounding; moss agate for increased immune functioning, happiness, and overall balance; and larimar for stillness, calm, and chilling vibes.

Feng Shui

For optimal feng shui balance and harmony: Clear all clutter; use earth and wood elements, such as teal, yellow, and brown colors; include plants and flowers for healing, growth, self-care, and boundaries.

20

TAKE TIME FOR TIME-OUT

There are times when we "do nothing" and it feels so guilty. As if we are disappointing someone. As if we are failing. As if we are lazy. Like we don't deserve a break. Like we are not worthy of using our time for ourselves. Like our time-out hurts someone else.

Wherever we learned this work ethic, it's wrong for most of us, and we are all suffering from it. Like a child who may benefit from a little solitude to break the tension and reflect on her actions, we all need to step back every now and then to "do nothing." So, take time for time-out. Doing nothing is actually one of the best things we can do. Holistic restoration is only possible with rest. This is how we honor ourselves.

Contrary to what it may seem like, we are not doing "nothing," but doing "something" very important and necessary. We are refreshing, recharging, reconnecting, and relaxing. Everyone needs this. Especially you.

Take a time-out wherever you are. By now, you should realize that you do not have to be in a dark, empty room to relax. On the contrary, you can be surrounded by beauty, luxury, and an environment full of life. Do what works for you.

Fight or flight? How about sip or soak instead? No one is "on" and available all the time. Try this instead:

- Set up office hours and don't work beyond them.
- Schedule your chilling-out shifts too. Get these on the calendar and stick to them.
- Get off the grind! Take your time off; you deserve it!

Decrease sickness, be your best, and increase your life span (yes!) by taking time for yourself.

Affirmation

> **I schedule my chill-out time, making space
> for myself in the day to just be.**

Holistic Prescription

 Call to Action

Unplug from technology. To unplug, simply turn off the computer, TV, tablet, and phone. Create a technology-free zone where you can exist with a focus on yourself and be comfortable without distractions. If necessary, practice ten minutes at a time.

 Mother Nature

Use these herbs: lavender for peaceful relaxation and restorative rest; chamomile for calming relaxation; and passionflower to reduce restlessness, anxiety, and insomnia.

 Gemstones

Activate these gemstones: howlite for remaining true to yourself and to soothe emotions; turquoise for health and inner calm; and larimar for stillness, calm, and chilling vibes.

 Feng Shui

For optimal feng shui balance and harmony: Clear all clutter in your home and work spaces; use soft lighting and textures where you like to relax; add earth elements like plants and soothing colors like yellow and beige for grounding and self-care; use water (baths, showers, swimming) to help you relax, heal, and let go.

21

MOVE YOUR BODY

Your body is meant to move. You can release and relax by slowing down with calming activities like journaling and meditation, but you can also have wonderfully cathartic releases by exercising.

During the most stressful, hectic times, exercise is the thing that tends to go first. However, this is exactly when it should be prioritized. It is exercise that can maintain your sanity. When trying times arrive, established workout routines can save you.

Exercise is stimulating, and it can help balance our emotional state by activating the "feel-good" chemicals and hormones in our bodies—for example, endorphins. In this way, exercise does so much more than fortify you physically. Exercise protects your entire being and can help you choose healthy coping behaviors, have pride in yourself, solve your most pressing problems, seek help, feel good about who you are, identify as a survivor rather than a victim, help others, find positive meaning in your experiences, and respond effectively despite feeling fear. Yes, all that!

When you choose to move your body, even during the most stressful times in your life, you are helping your mind, body, and spirit to rise, reset, and recover. The cycle of moving your body, chilling out, and in-between is just what you need for strengthening, conditioning, and toning for optimal health.

Yes, yoga is exercise. Same with dancing, walking, gardening, roller-skating, sex, and any enjoyable physical activity that gets your heart pumping, is all considered exercise. You can reap similar benefits from doing them as you do with jogging on a treadmill or doing Pilates. To maximize this process, it is important to remember a few things: First, exercise is not supposed to feel like punishment! Instead, gently push yourself within your extended comfort zone. Also avoid comparing yourself to and competing against others. Claim your space, a dedicated time and place to move your body, a personal domain that you create just for you. It's your body. You can move it any way you like.

Affirmation

My body feels great when it moves, so I make sure I exercise in a fun way at least three times a week.

Holistic Prescription

 Call to Action

Choose movement activities that you enjoy; you will find that you will do them more often and more consistently. The mental health and physical benefits will be greater too.

 Mother Nature

Use these herbs: peppermint for enhanced healing, luck, love, and protection; thyme for spiritual awareness, plus healing with love and courage; and clove for physical stimulation and positive energy attraction.

 Gemstones

Activate these gemstones: bloodstone for increased physical strength and vitality; tiger's eye for increasing confidence while releasing fear and anxiety; and turquoise for health and inner calm.

 Feng Shui

For optimal feng shui balance and harmony: Add wood elements, such as trees and plants, plus yellow and orange earth colors for self-care, inspiration, and vitality; add metal elements, such as metal furnishings and accents, for joy and beauty; add the fire color red for stimulation.

22

STIMULATE ENDORPHINS

Endorphins are chemicals in your brain that make you feel superb. I love endorphins. Repeat: I *love* endorphins. Yes, I know what you are probably thinking: Sex releases endorphins. But fortunately, exercise also releases endorphins!

Maybe you are not presently in a position to pursue sex safely with someone else, but you can almost always easily pleasure yourself or exercise. Endorphins decrease physical, emotional, and mental tension. They help you sleep better and can even enhance a positive mood. Releasing endorphins, then, becomes a great facilitator for relaxation and letting go. Who knew? (Well…some of us did.)

And here is a bonus, a little-known fact: Endorphins also help increase emotional resilience. Resilience is what helps you cope with trauma and difficult situations of all kinds. When you have resilience, you can deal with negative people and circumstances, and slights roll off you quickly and easily without internalization. You can recover from life's challenges much faster. Resilience gives us the ability to cope and provides protection against the disruptions caused by the changes we all face.

With endorphins, you are in a better position to handle life. Consider some of the protective factors associated with resilience and recovery:

- Identifying as a survivor rather than a victim
- Healthy coping behaviors
- Strong cultural identity and ethnic pride
- Effective problem-solving skills and help-seeking
- Internal locus of control
- Connections with family and friends
- Self-disclosure and finding positive meaning in trauma
- Feeling good about one's own actions in the face of danger
- Spirituality and helping others
- Being able to respond effectively despite feeling fear

Get your spirit glowing and your heart pumping with endorphins. It makes a difference. It works.

Affirmation

I release my feel-good endorphins often and bask in the glow.

Holistic Prescription

 Call to Action

Through your own process of self-discovery, find the best ways to release endorphins.

 Mother Nature

Use these herbs: green tea for physical body regulation; rosemary for physical healing; and lemon balm for physical restoration.

 Gemstones

Activate these gemstones: carnelian for strength, self-worth, and confidence; pyrite for transformative healing; and onyx for absorbing and transforming negative energy, plus increasing emotional and physical strength.

 Feng Shui

For optimal feng shui balance and harmony: Add earth and fire elements for self-care, inspiration, and vitality; include red and pink colors to promote passion; add metal elements like mirrors and metal artwork and furniture for joy and beauty.

23

UPLIFT YOUR BODY

No one's body is the same. Put the same outfit on twenty different women and it will look completely different on each one. We honor this uniqueness that has been years in the making. The key is to claim, love, and take care of *your* body.

Your body is a temple. Also, a divine vessel. And a tool. Plus, a mode of expression and communication. It is a physical representation of our spiritual selves. Some would argue that your body is a finite and temporary creation. Whether you think this or not, your body is here. You are here and it's yours. So, it has infinite value.

Still, sometimes we feel "out of it." There are times in our lives when we are in need of some *upliftment*. You don't have to suffer from a physical disability or athletic injury for your body to feel broken, sluggish, unloved, unused, and in need of rejuvenation.

When you cherish your body, you uplift it. Hold your head high! Hold your body with great posture and be proud of what your body does for you. Not to be confused with body image, uplifting your body has nothing to do with how you feel about what you look like (maybe you can change that too). You uplift it when you:

- Love your body.
- Move your body regularly.
- Detox your body and cleanse your aura.
- Maintain good hygiene.
- Eat high-quality, nutrient-dense foods.
- Prioritize loving touch.
- Pamper yourself.

You uplift your body to cherish it and treat it with the love and care that is required to make chilling out a priority; you are putting your body in a special category and not taking it for granted. If you don't uplift your body and love it, you are more disconnected from it and fail to honor its needs.

Affirmation

I love my body and I fully appreciate all that it does for me.

Holistic Prescription

 Call to Action

Use meditative exercises like yoga and walking to help release endorphins and remove toxins.

 Mother Nature

Use these herbs and flowers: rosemary for purified physical healing love; cedarwood for positive new beginnings; and honeysuckle for beauty, personal power, and self-love.

 Gemstones

Activate these gemstones: ruby for healing and positive energy recovery; hematite for physical healing; and aventurine for nurturing yourself, bringing joy, and a positive attitude.

 Feng Shui

For optimal feng shui balance and harmony: Add metal furnishings for joy and beauty; add a circular water element for connection; add the color red and sunshine for vitality (fire element).

24

CREATE PHYSICAL EXPERIENCES

If you are tired of going to the doctor for medication or the hospital for surgery, get physical instead. It's like trick or treat. Would you rather wait to deal with an illness or prevent it? Do you want a trick, or do you want a treat?

Maybe you don't think of yourself as a "physical" person. That doesn't matter so much. We are all physical, each in our own way. Which way do you like best? Think about what gets you excited. When your heart races, that is from adrenaline. It means you are alive and in touch with yourself and your body barometers. Let's make it a joyful rush, filled with excitement and curiosity—one that you can tap in to over and over again at will.

When you are thinking about moving your body, don't hesitate. Don't be afraid to get sweaty. Feel good knowing that when you sweat, you are also detoxing. Don't forget to replenish with plenty of water. Now, your body is ready to chill out.

You can start this process right away by running, jogging, cycling, or lifting weights, but also by dancing, walking, gardening, intense touching, sex, and any enjoyable physical activity that gets your heart pumping. What else do you want to do? You can try something different. Don't resist your animal urge to run, jump, play, bounce, kick, or punch. It's there. Maybe deep inside. But it's there.

Getting physical alone is great, but doing so with others can help keep you motivated, along with other benefits. It's no small wonder: When you exercise with a significant other, you are also infusing loving vibrations and (fun!) endorphins. What is more divine than increasing cardiovascular health while activating your heart chakra at the same time? Whether you do so by yourself or with others, you will immediately sense the benefits. A reminder: Sex is getting physical too.

Affirmation

I move my body on a regular basis, feeling good, healthy, and free.

Holistic Prescription

 Call to Action

Go outside at least three times each day for a minimum of ten minutes to observe the trees, smell the air, and move your body.

 Mother Nature

Use these herbs and flowers: cinnamon for grounding and balancing energy; jasmine for self-worth, beauty, and spiritual awareness; and juniper berries for releasing negativity.

 Gemstones

Activate these gemstones: jade for wisdom, peace, heart energy, and harmony; onyx for absorbing and transforming negative energy, plus increasing emotional and physical strength; and aquamarine to clear the mind and connect to higher health and well-being.

 Feng Shui

For optimal feng shui balance and harmony: Add fire elements like the red and fiery orange colors, plus sunshine for inspiration, dynamic energy, and vitality.

25

REACH OUT AND TOUCH

Being touch-deprived presents itself as a different type of loneliness. A lot of times, we don't even know how to identify it, and it might not always be clear that this is why we are suffering. When we reach out and touch each other, we do more than we realize: We are optimizing our health using the power of touch. Even for generally private people, regular physical connection with family and a small group of friends is helpful.

During the coronavirus pandemic, we did what we were advised to do. We sheltered in place and restricted physical contact. If you lived alone with just your dog, you were grateful for that dog! When we were with people to whom we no longer felt a genuine connection, that became obvious too. When we did go out for essential tasks like grocery shopping, we did so socially distanced, staying away from others. We self-isolated.

This type of separation began to take a toll not only on our psyches but also on our physical selves. Are you a "people person" who missed people? If you are, chances are, telephone and video contact only seemed to make things worse. It would not be surprising to become frustrated and lacking in energy from being touch-deprived.

How do you know if you are touch-deprived? You will probably begin to fantasize about hugging, cuddling, and the warmth of a physical body next to you in bed. Although your thoughts are not necessarily sexual, they are definitely physical and flesh-inspired. Maybe you fell in love with your neighbor or did other things—no judgment here!

We need what we need. It's not wrong to get what you want and need, as long as you are not hurting someone or being hurt in the process. If you are not being touched in a loving way on a regular basis by your partner, know that you deserve to be with someone who wants to touch you, likes to touch you often, and will do whatever they can to please you. Hopefully, you have that or can develop it in your life.

Affirmation

> I am comfortable with my body and my need to give and receive sensual pleasures like touching.

Holistic Prescription

Call to Action

Don't be shy in exploring your body, especially your skin. Practice touch and related physical sensations, doing what feels safe for you, and then, exploring your touch boundaries even more.

Mother Nature

Use these herbs and flowers: honeysuckle for beauty, personal power, and self-love; rose for increasing love vibrations, including self-love; and rosemary for purified physical healing love.

Gemstones

Activate these gemstones: rose quartz for warm, caring, gentle self-love and emotional healing by releasing resentments; garnet for chi stimulation and to remove emotional blockages in the body; and rhodonite for stimulating, clearing, and activating the heart.

Feng Shui

For optimal feng shui balance and harmony: Add more yin (feminine) items that are soft and fluffy and feel good against your skin; clear all clutter in your home and eliminate as many electronics as possible from your bedroom; add fire elements by using candles for positive scents and romantic lighting and the color red for passion.

26

BEAUTIFY YOUR LIFE

Beauty and wellness go hand in hand. To be elegant and sexy, we must be healthy: physically, mentally, and spiritually. Holistic health helps you be even more beautiful. Chilling out helps you stay that way.

In addition to touch, some of us became obsessed with beauty during the pandemic: enhancing the beauty in our home and the beauty in ourselves. Did you spend countless hours redecorating your space? Maybe you painted the whole house. It was awesome! Or was it just me? Perhaps you began new self-care practices for your skin, hair, nails, and body after realizing that you *needed* this beauty in your life. If you became the queen of beauty product deliveries, find comfort in knowing that you were not the only one.

Metaphysically, beauty evokes strong, positive energy vibrations that have physical effects on our biological bodies. I would argue that beauty, love, and touch are not simply desired to enrich our lives—they are essential to our health and emotional well-being. This is especially true during times of crisis but also consistent with how we, as human beings, generally operate.

Touch, beauty, and love are as necessary as breathing.

Your idea of beauty does not need to match anyone else's, because it's yours. You may find beauty in the mundane, the unusual, or something else. It doesn't matter whether you already have it or you acquire it, and there is no need to spend any money to beautify—it's about honoring the beauty in everything starting with yourself.

Love yourself to invest in *you*, especially your beauty. Insist on beautification. It is what you deserve.

Affirmation

When I take care of myself, I honor my beauty within, which also helps me create a beautiful home as a place where I belong.

Holistic Prescription

 Call to Action

Identify what is uniquely gorgeous about your skin, your face, your hair, then maybe move onto the furnishings in your home. There is inspiration in that chair, your favorite plate, the lighting.

 Mother Nature

Use these plants: jasmine for self-worth, beauty, and spiritual awareness; aloe vera for soothing physical healing properties; and turmeric for detoxing, refreshing, and brightening.

 Gemstones

Activate these gemstones: carnelian for strength, self-worth, and confidence; tiger's eye for increasing confidence while releasing fear and anxiety; and labradorite for intuition and to protect your aura.

 Feng Shui

For optimal feng shui balance and harmony: Incorporate all the natural feng shui elements that bring you great joy (water, wood, earth, metal, fire); clear the clutter in your home and edit your furnishings to make your most beautiful objects stand out and shine; keep dust to a minimum; use open spaces and cross breezes, plants, and flowers to bring in the outdoors.

27

LEARN TO SOOTHE YOURSELF

Where you find comfort and peace is your sacred space. In this space, you can take good care of yourself and protect your psyche from external chaos. You can do this anywhere and anytime when you know how to soothe yourself.

We all need soothing. Babies learn to do it during infancy. Over the last couple of years you have probably learned more about what you need in this area.

What do you do to soothe yourself? Here are some ideas:

- Try creating a soothing work space. You can do this, even if it's just a corner of a room, a piece of furniture, or a special spot in the yard.
- Also…use your words. Amazingly, we have the power to soothe ourselves by what we say to ourselves and how we say it. So, revisit your words. The way that we talk to others is important but not as important as how we talk to ourselves. A soothing statement or affirmation can soothe you in unimaginable ways. Positive self-talk like this changes your brain waves and creates happiness, even during times of grief and darkness. So simple, yet so powerful and effective. It is soothing self-talk that you can rely on to lift yourself up at any time. Repeat as needed.
- You can also soothe yourself by being grateful. Revisit your actions. Telling yourself what you are joyful about and what you have gratitude for is a simple and effective way to lift your spirits and reinforce the fact that you are okay and that this, too, shall pass. You know, things could be so much worse. Expressing gratitude is a balancing action. It moves you closer to your divine destiny, which is one of peace, greatness, and joy.

Affirmation

I soothe myself during stressful times and do it regularly to maintain my comfort and balance.

Holistic Prescription

 Call to Action

Keep a gratitude journal, a book dedicated to expressing what you are grateful for, that you can reference and add to during times of distress.

 Mother Nature

Use these herbs: sage for spiritual purification and new positive beginnings; lavender for peaceful relaxation and restorative rest; and valerian root for enhanced quality of rest.

 Gemstones

Activate these gemstones: amber for soothing and inspiring a carefree, optimistic disposition; jade for wisdom, peace, heart energy, and harmony; and unakite for removing negativity and balancing emotions.

 Feng Shui

For optimal feng shui balance and harmony: Clear clutter for a more soothing environment; use soothing colors like white, gray, and yellow; add earth and wood elements—for example, wooden furnishings and plants—to enhance self-care and healing; add a water element—for example, a fountain to create an environment with soothing sounds.

28

CREATE A HEART-FILLED LIFE

Love sets you free.

Some of us give away our love so deeply and completely that we forget to save some for ourselves. Rather than lose yourself in love, let it take you higher.

The foundation for healthy relationships with others is self-love. Without it, you are left feeling depleted, empty, and exhausted. Don't despair…you can take it back!

In fact, you *must* take it back, because as the song "Very Special" by Debra Laws says, "love is life and life is living." Take back your most special and unique loving energy by starting from within: self-love and self-care. We create love in our lives by prioritizing first self-love and then self-care. By loving ourselves, we place our own care above the needs of others. It becomes the deep well from which others can draw.

It is possible to create a heart-filled life without compromise or regret.

Enhance your love life by filling your sacred heart space with loving energy, images, and light to create an aura so bright, strong, and beautiful that you instantly become a love beacon, attracting all kinds of love. It's all coming to you, so…be selective.

People who need people are often looking for love. Surround yourself with love to reactivate your *anahata* or heart chakra. Your mission, should you choose to accept it, is to heal, protect, and keep your *anahata* vibrating at a high frequency. This is the key to all loving relationships. Without it, we fail to give love fully and completely, and we are unable to fully and completely accept love, including self-love.

Affirmation

I embrace love in all of its forms, bringing me light, brightness, and joy.

Holistic Prescription

 Call to Action

Read books, watch movies, and engage in media sources that promote healthy, loving relationships between family, friends, and significant others.

 Mother Nature

Use these herbs, flowers, and natural substances to create a heart-filled life: honeysuckle for beauty, personal power, and self-love; rose for increasing love vibrations including self-love; and honey to enhance sweetness.

 Gemstones

Activate these gemstones: rose quartz for warm, caring, gentle self-love and emotional healing by releasing resentments; garnet for chi stimulation and to remove emotional blockages in the body; and aventurine to bring joy, acceptance, and well-being.

 Feng Shui

For optimal feng shui balance and harmony: Add more soft, yin (feminine) items and use pink, red, and white colors in and around your home; add symmetrical pairs of items—for example, two chairs and two nightstands—to encourage romantic pairings; add metal furnishings and gold/silver/copper metallic colors to increase joy, love, and beauty in your home.

29

EAT WELL

Craving chocolate, pizza, potato chips, or macaroni and cheese is not a crime. Women cannot live off salad alone. But why be a woman who eats to live when you can be one who eats well to live well? Eating is often a cultural and communal experience. For some, eating delicious food can even be described as spiritual enlightenment. This is no coincidence. During ancient and historical times, group bonding from hunting, gathering, serving, and eating together benefited everyone.

When you love yourself, you care and make better choices. Most of us realize that if you fill yourself with junk food, you become junky. If you fill yourself with health food, you become healthy. But, there's more. Eating well is not just what you eat; it's also *how* you eat. The key is chilling out.

A rushed lifestyle often includes rushed meals. A rushed meal is harmful in so many ways. It adds stress to a daily task that we are required to do for basic survival. Stress encourages poor food choices that prioritize rapid energy highs, fleeting feelings of comfort, and convenience over health. Stress interferes with digestion and ultimately wreaks havoc on the body.

As social beings, whenever possible, we should sit down with others to eat in picturesque settings. Because quality matters, eat organic foods. Portion and bite sizes matter too. You can choose smaller plates and split larger meals into two or three meals. Take smaller bites and chew your food longer to help your body digest it. When you slow down, you allow your body to catch up (you are more likely to realize when you are no longer hungry).

So, you can slow down to focus on your food. What's the hurry? Your body is probably already telling you that it's time to make the time. It means prioritizing sit-down meals, flavors, and portions. It means respecting the digestion process. And it means choosing quality over quantity.

Chilling out to enjoy your food is not a chore but can be an uplifting event. You can't help but relax and chill out when presented with bountiful delicious offerings in a calm, serene setting. Don't rush... instead, savor it.

Above all, be happy when you eat—enjoy!

Affirmation

I eat well for my holistic benefit.

Holistic Prescription

 Call to Action

From seed to harvest to preparation and presentation, show appreciation and gratitude for the plants and animals that have been sacrificed so that you can be well nourished, and be thankful to the folks growing, selling, cooking, and serving your food.

 Mother Nature

Use these herbs: green tea for physical body regulation; chamomile for calming relaxation; and parsley for detoxification.

 Gemstones

Activate these gemstones: hematite for physical healing; moss agate for increased immune functioning, happiness, and overall balance; and bloodstone for increased physical strength and vitality.

 Feng Shui

For optimal feng shui balance and harmony: Focus on earth tones with yellow, orange, beige, and tan colors for self-care; focus on wood elements with herbal potted plants, wooden utensils and bowls, and wood tones with green, blue, and turquoise colors.

30

USE STILLNESS AS YOUR SUPERPOWER

Sometimes it feels like the world is moving so fast around us. There's so much pressure to rush around and be like other people. You start to question your reality. Are you doing what you are supposed to be doing? Are you, really?

Try not to compare yourself to others. Let them scurry around. Your stillness is your superpower.

Maybe you've been moving full speed ahead for many years now. Have you ever been told that you need to relax more? Did it come from a place of love and support, or a from a place of contempt or underappreciation? Many women are told to relax. But my advice to you, dear reader, is coming from a place of love and support. I want you to be healthy and whole. I want your body to function the way it is designed to, and I want each of your days to feel great. My wishes for you are all about balancing productivity with your rest and relaxation.

We don't always need to be moving to be productive. Busyness is not the same as progress. By being mindful, we can make big impacts in all areas of our lives. And someone observing us from the outside may not even notice.

Contrary to popular opinion, relaxing is not shutting anything down. It is tapping within to redirect and bring something out. Relaxation is both an art and a science. If you get too technical with it, you lose the artfulness, what makes it special and unique for you.

Some of us need to get out of our own way and stop making ourselves sick. Relaxation is, in some ways, a manifestation of patience. It is allowing what is supposed to happen, what *will* happen, to happen. It is natural, not forced, though it can be scheduled until you get used to letting it occur naturally on its own.

Affirmation

During my most challenging times, as well as in times of divine bliss, I am aware, alert, and still.

Holistic Prescription

 Call to Action

Actively resist the urge to fill up all your time with activities. Instead, schedule time for "stillness."

 Mother Nature

Use these herbs to promote stillness: allspice for self-awareness, emotional healing, and luck; clove for physical stimulation and positive energy attraction; and chamomile for calming relaxation.

 Gemstones

Activate these gemstones: howlite for remaining true to yourself and to soothe emotions; aventurine to bring joy, acceptance, and well-being; and larimar for stillness, calm, and chilling vibes.

 Feng Shui

For optimal feng shui balance and harmony: Use earth colors like tan and yellow; add green and teal colors to promote stillness; add wood elements like furniture to promote knowledge and stability and plants for grounding; add water elements like circles and blue colors for calm.

Part Two

MIND

What you think is key. What you say is important. What you do in your everyday life matters. This is your mind in action.

Your mind is an amazing asset. No matter how high your IQ may be, most human beings only use a very small percentage of the brain's potential. Still, ironically, that doesn't stop us from overthinking and overanalyzing even simple situations. Other times, we let our mind's reasoning power get overshadowed by our intense emotions.

To make matters more confusing, we are constantly being bombarded by information and, sometimes, misinformation. It can be difficult to know what sources to listen to and whom to trust. This confusion creates constant noise, even if it is in the background, which makes what to do less clear. Too much internal conflict leads to chaos and anxiety.

It's scary not always knowing what to do or what to expect. Even positive change can produce anxiety if you let it, but don't run away. Instead, embrace the possibilities. Learn to use your mind to choose expansion over confusion.

In Part 2, you will learn to drive the CAR—a simple and effective strategy for balancing mental conflict. In addition, you'll learn other strategies like how to parent yourself, accept change, act in your best interest, be more than your feelings, and more.

31

DRIVE THE CAR

Our world has been through some huge changes on a global scale. New information creates daily change in the ecosystem; yesterday is not like today, and today is not like tomorrow. Our environment changes, and we change too.

The three stages to attaining peace and balance can be summarized as CAR:

- **C**hange acceptance
- **A**daptive action
- **R**elaxation and letting go

After a life change, we are encouraged to do things differently. This is *change acceptance*, which simply means accepting a change event. It can be major, subtle, or extreme. Change acceptance can be the hardest step. However, if you never accept the change event, you will likely remain stuck in crisis mode. If you are unable to move through the three stages, your capacity to adapt, relax, and let go is virtually impossible. If you continue to internalize the information and fail to utilize that information to change your behavior for your greater good, you will stay off-balance. Let's move forward! Don't stay stuck, existing in a state of passively receiving and reacting, all input with no process or output. Don't be a zombie! Change acceptance may be difficult, but once you do it and move on, everything will thank you.

Acceptance of the change event is the foundation for the next stage, *adaptive action*. Only after we accept the change can we move forward to adaptive action. We can only begin to adapt when we accept that the way we did things before is now over. We must recognize that letting go of the old is necessary to usher in the new. Although some people may be slow to adapt or refuse to adapt at all, this understanding is required to move to the next stage, *relaxation and letting go* of old behaviors.

When we engage in this process, it takes power away from others and puts it where it belongs—squarely on you. Relaxation and letting go challenges the status quo. It dares you to take charge of your life to embrace a holistic lifestyle, get in the CAR, and drive it!

Affirmation

I adapt easily to change, knowing that it supports my highest good.

Holistic Prescription

 ### Call to Action
Be prepared for change as the expectation of a good life.

 ### Mother Nature
Use these herbs: skullcap for releasing and relinquishing control; thyme for spiritual awareness, plus healing with love and courage; and cedarwood for positive new beginnings.

 ### Gemstones
Activate these gemstones: blue agate for patience, peace, hope, and positive thinking; fluorite for peace and increasing mental clarity; and lapis for wisdom and serene awareness.

 ### Feng Shui
For optimal feng shui balance and harmony: Use candles and the color red for adaptive change; use wood elements such as wooden furnishings and plants for growth and healing; use the water color blue for wisdom and connection.

32

STOP LIVING IN CHAOS

Just because you may not see your chaos doesn't mean that it's not there. Maybe it hides behind busyness, obligations, responsibilities, restlessness, or fear. Are you always on the go? Do you feel tired most of the time? Do you have difficulties "turning off" your brain? A mind that is constantly active is fighting itself, creating internal conflict and a lifestyle in which the body and spirit rarely rest either.

Let's stop hurting ourselves.

Your mind, body, and spirit in a state of chaos is not sustainable. It keeps you from focusing on your purpose—what's truly important—and from seeing the life choices that add value. It causes energy stagnation and illness.

We live. We rest.

Chilling out is your secret weapon. Stop. Breathe. Let go.

I know that you understand that being well is not just about eating the healthiest foods and exercising. It's a mental state, a daily state of emotional well-being, feeling hopeful. It's about how you process your past experiences, holding onto them or letting them go. Sometimes, you may need a gentle reminder about what you do with your time, energy, and talents in service to yourself and the world. Here, it is, with the utmost respect, to help you heal.

Your healing process, as long as it takes, wherever it takes you, may be uncomfortable, especially at first. But if you hide from the feelings of unfamiliarity, you can never get used to the process of healing and the wonderful feeling of being healed.

Affirmation

> **When I start to feel anxious, I remember to stop, breathe, and let go.**

Holistic Prescription

 Call to Action
Instead of hiding from healing with chaos, open up to it and welcome its relief.

 Mother Nature
Use these herbs: bay leaves for spiritual enhancement and protection; cinnamon for grounding and balancing energy; and juniper berries for releasing negativity.

 Gemstones
Activate these gemstones: aventurine for nurturing yourself, bringing joy and a positive attitude; turquoise for health and inner calm; and howlite for remaining true to yourself and to soothe emotions.

 Feng Shui
For optimal feng shui balance and harmony: Clear all clutter; use earth and wood elements such as teal, yellow, and brown colors; add plants and flowers for healing, growth, self-care, and boundaries.

33

LEARN TO PARENT YOURSELF

What does it take to be a good parent? Some may say it is love, patience, and TLC. What would happen if you treated yourself like an excellent parent would treat their child?

When you think about what you learned from your parents, you may have mixed emotions of joy, sadness, disappointment, and pride. Most of our parents did something that we vow to do differently. Yet, here we are, so they must have done something right. Vow to do differently with yourself, and vow to do right too.

How would you encourage your child? Lift her up and teach her to recover from bad times and not dwell on the past? Show her that mistakes are just part of learning? How will you instill in her the notion that she can do anything she dreams of doing, that she can heal and recover from personal loss, that she is smart and capable, funny, and unconditionally adored?

When you learn to do this for yourself, you will attain a new level of self-love and self-care that some folks can only dream of: parenting yourself.

Like a child, you are always learning from your mistakes and gaining wisdom along the way. Now, you can treat yourself with that compassion. Be gentle. Be kind. Here are just a few of the ways to parent yourself:

- When you mess up, be gentle with yourself and do something to make yourself feel better.
- When you fall down, encourage yourself to get back up and try again.
- If today was difficult, remind yourself that tomorrow is a brand new day.
- When you are at your wit's end, allow a short tantrum (five minutes or less), then get it together.
- Run a bath for yourself to relax. Don't forget the bubbles!

Affirmation

I love and nurture the little girl in me like a beautiful, loving, generous parent.

Holistic Prescription

 Call to Action

Every day, give yourself a hug and a kiss. Tell yourself how special you are.

 Mother Nature

Use these herbs and flowers: rose for increasing love vibrations, including self-love; thyme for spiritual awareness, plus healing with love and courage; yarrow for raising the frequency of love vibrations.

 Gemstones

Activate these gemstones: rose quartz for warm, caring, gentle self-love and emotional healing by releasing resentments; aventurine for nurturing yourself, bringing joy and a positive attitude; and carnelian for strength, self-worth, and confidence.

 Feng Shui

For optimal feng shui balance and harmony: Add water elements—for example, a circular table with chairs—to increase wisdom and connection; add earth elements—for example, yellow, orange, and beige colors—for grounding and self-care; add wood elements—for example, plants and flowers, wood furnishings, and green and blue colors for growth and healing.

34

TUNE OUT TROUBLES

Sometimes, even when we pride ourselves with how productive we are, we can get overwhelmed by deadlines, expectations, issues in our personal relationships, and the problems of the world. However, you can always tune in to tune out troubles.

You may wonder how you became too busy. It is not your fault. This was learned behavior, most likely from your parents. There may even be childhood trauma that affects your present inability to relax. In addition, you were very likely rewarded for doing so much for so many. Now, as a fully functioning adult aspiring to optimize your health, you can decide to live your life differently if you want to, free of unwanted entanglements.

When we learn more about who and what we are, we can master the technique of blocking external stimuli. Mostly, it is a shift in focus from external to internal. Instead of taking pride in doing so much for others, let's take pride in prioritizing and taking care of ourselves. And that glass must be half full, not half empty! Tuning in to tune out is an essential and learnable skill.

Although we are all affected by external stimuli, such as events of the world, relaxation is an internal process. The power of chilling out is real. What we surround ourselves with in creating our own trouble-free zone is critical in this process.

Regardless of what activities are going on around you, your mind and spirit are powerful. The physical sensations within your body and your spirit are wise barometers of comfort, pain, and distress. What are they saying? In what areas of your body do you have distress, an indicator of internalized chaos?

Tuning in to tune out is about choosing where to put your energy. Focus less on the external and more on you. Yes, you can focus on your own self to relax, let go, and live a healthy life, no matter what is going on. When you tune in to a peaceful state of chilling out, you can tune out any and all chaotic distractions.

Tuning out troubles to chill out makes you more productive, healthier, and a better person to be around.

Affirmation

I maintain a stable and peaceful state to keep troubles away and help me achieve my greatest dreams.

Holistic Prescription

 Call to Action

Recognize someone else's drama as a distraction so that you can ignore it. Just leave it alone!

 Mother Nature

Use these herbs: allspice for self-awareness, emotional healing, and luck; green tea for physical body regulation; and clove for physical stimulation and positive energy attraction.

 Gemstones

Activate these gemstones: citrine for enhanced manifestation, personal will, and prosperity; jade for wisdom, peace, heart energy, and harmony; and labradorite for intuition and to protect your aura.

 Feng Shui

For optimal feng shui balance and harmony: Create a sanctuary; clear all the clutter in your home; create open spaces and cross breezes for air flow; use plants and flowers for grounding and beauty; add yin (feminine) elements for self-care and nurturing; add wood furnishings for growth and healing.

35

ACTIVATE YOUR MIND AND SPIRIT

Have you ever tasted something so delicious that it blows your mind? Compliments to the chef! Take that feeling and apply it to something you did or created. Not feeling it yet? Try applying that feeling to a task you plan to do or a project you will create. That feeling of blowing your mind is because your mind and spirit are activated.

While you were doing you today, did you blow your mind?

Your journey within is the one that matters. Be proud of what you do and your accomplishments. Your thoughtful creativity, hard work, sweat, and tears created something magnificent, a brilliant representation. It will blow someone's mind, but first make sure it does so for you.

When it does, you are connecting yourself to your soul purpose in a way that can be life-changing, affirming, and absolutely beautiful. A unification of mind, spirit, and action. Your mind and spirit are highly energetic. Your body too. You need positive energy for positive change. It's there. If you need it now, activate it now.

Once you are awakened, when you are at one with yourself, you needn't worry about doing great things. You can chill out *and* excel. You will know it happens when your life path:

- Is authentic
- Comes naturally and easily to you
- Feels like you "must" do it
- Brings you peace
- Brings you joy

Affirmation

In the process of creating greatness, in service and in rest,
I am united in mind, body, and spirit.

Holistic Prescription

 Call to Action

Raise the bar. Instead of accepting things that are okay, make them shine with excellence. Remember to chill out in the process.

 Mother Nature

Use these herbs and flowers: jasmine for self-worth, beauty, and spiritual awareness; thyme for spiritual awareness, plus healing with love and courage; and bay leaves for spiritual enhancement and protection.

 Gemstones

Activate these gemstones: amethyst for fortification and spiritual awareness; lapis for wisdom and serene awareness; and aventurine for nurturing yourself, bringing joy, and a positive attitude.

 Feng Shui

For optimal feng shui balance and harmony: Clear clutter; add wood elements like plants and flowers, especially roses to increase vitality and growth; add fire with red accents for confidence and dynamic energy; add water elements like black and blue colors for deep wisdom.

36

RELEASE CHILDHOOD TRAUMA

Releasing your childhood identity means making a distinct break from your old self. It is challenging, because your identity is what you have been holding onto for so long. Repeating trauma may seem "normal." But is your identity a current one, or is it a reflection of the past, maybe even from when you were a child?

As healthy, adult women, we cannot act, function, or see ourselves as little girls or as victims. We are survivors. Letting go of your past identity as a child is the key to reclaiming who you are as an adult.

I apologize for how some people may have hurt you when you were a child. I'm sorry that they neglected to be there for you when you needed them the most. I hurt when any child suffers. It affects all of us. If you grew up around unhealthy, even violent, people, at some point, the little girl in you was full of despair. You didn't have control over your environment, where to be, and how long to stay there. You lacked the autonomy to leave when things got bad.

Now, as a functioning adult, you can make choices that the little girl couldn't. You are not stuck. You are not anybody's victim. You are in control. Take back your life. Take back your power.

Even if you are not a particularly sensitive or empathetic person, you still probably absorb and hold onto emotionally charged experiences much more than you should. Are you feeling gloomy from the turmoil of the past? Do you score high with Adverse Childhood Experiences (ACEs) in the ACEs survey (https://sisterhoodagenda .com/are-aces-putting-you-at-risk)? Do you relive these childhood traumas on a regular basis?

You are so much more than a statistic, and, yes, you always knew that you deserved better. Release the bad now to embrace your positive reality. Now, with greater resilience, you can create whatever you want to. But first…you have to let it go. Distress outside your body creates distress inside your body if you do not properly protect yourself. We can and should release our childhood trauma to be healthy adults.

Affirmation

I am more than what happened to me as a little girl. As an empowered woman, I create my own destiny.

Holistic Prescription

 Call to Action

Write the names of those who hurt you as a child on a piece of paper and burn it (see entry 90: Burn It).

 Mother Nature

Use these plants: sage for spiritual purification and new positive beginnings; honeysuckle for beauty, personal power, and self-love; and lime to promote healing that prioritizes love.

 Gemstones

Activate these gemstones: petrified wood for purification and grounding; rhodochrosite for emotional healing from childhood trauma and reclaiming self; and rhodonite for emotional clearing from shock, trauma, and emotional wounds to achieve balance, self-love, and self-compassion.

 Feng Shui

For optimal feng shui balance and harmony: Clear all clutter; remove anything that reminds you of a painful past experience; add a small water fountain to help things flow onward and move on; add earth and wood elements, such as plants and flowers and white, green, and blue colors, for grounding and healing; surround yourself with beauty and graceful (yin) objects that celebrate the feminine, such as flowing, billowy curtains and satin sheets; add wood furnishings for growth and healing.

37

PREVENT DESPAIR

Challenges can make or break your rhythm. But they don't have to break *you*. A break in rhythm is not a broken spirit. Darkness rooted in hopelessness feeds off despair and sadness. Don't let mistakes or a wrong turn uproot your whole life! Forgive any mistakes. It's okay because, as the saying goes, nobody's perfect.

Good can come out of the bad (yes, it can). Challenges are opportunities to rise. This is exactly when we must remember to accept what is and remain hopeful. Acceptance is not giving up; it's letting go to move on with your life. Acceptance and having hope, even when you don't see or feel great, are the keys to preventing despair.

Time heals. With hope, always give it time. Moving on shows bravery and great strength in the face of challenging adversities. It prevents despair from annihilating your soul. Take it one day at a time. Or one hour at a time. One minute…one second at a time. The more you wait, the farther away the issue goes. Leave it in the rearview. Give yourself more time to balance your emotions and the Universe more time to create solutions on your behalf.

There are always options. As an empowered woman, I know that, yes, even you, may need to be reminded that you have choices. This means that resolutions are near and never far away.

Remember. Remember not to freak out. Remember who and what you are. Remember that this, too, shall pass. And remember to never ever give up.

Acceptance and hope take you toward the light. Continue to dream of better. Of more. Of fabulous tomorrows, that, by definition, will be different from today.

Affirmation

Holistic Prescription

 Call to Action

If you don't like where you are in your life, use hope to give you the fuel to move forward (with a good plan!) in the spirit of positive change.

 Mother Nature

Use these herbs: chamomile for calming relaxation; cedarwood for positive new beginnings; and thyme for spiritual awareness, plus healing with love and courage.

 Gemstones

Activate these gemstones: tiger's eye for increasing confidence while releasing fear and anxiety; selenite for dispelling negative energy; and lepidolite for attracting love, hope, and light, plus change acceptance.

 Feng Shui

For optimal feng shui balance and harmony: Use earth elements for grounding; use green, blue, and teal colors to promote relaxation and calm; add water elements by visiting water sources, such as oceans, rivers, and lakes, for relaxation and letting go, and to increase connection to the world.

38

ACCEPT CHANGE

Did you ever have trouble opening something? A task that you did every day without a thought suddenly became quite impossible. I bet you got a bit frustrated, put a lot of effort into it, and made several more attempts. It still wouldn't open, huh? If you took a break (and a few deep breaths)…voilà! It opened effortlessly like magic. You got the outcome that you desired only after you stopped trying so hard to make it work.

Life works like that too. It's time to stop fighting change and start surrendering to it.

Contrary to popular belief, trying very hard to get to our desired outcome is not always the best way to get what we want. Sometimes we have to pause, step away, and rebalance ourselves first. Like when you struggle to remember something and you can't, no matter how hard you try. Then later, when you are doing something else, the information suddenly comes to you and you recall it without any effort at all.

Accepting change works just that way.

To achieve a harmonious state, we must understand that this balanced equilibrium is neither still nor silent, but an active natural state of being, like balancing on a tightrope or the changing seasons. When it's accomplished in a healthy way, it looks effortless and appears right on time.

Sometimes change and progress looks like instability. Acknowledging instability and being okay with it means admitting the natural flow of life, which is motion and change. As we accept ourselves as a part of the natural world, we accept what is.

Being open-minded to what change looks like can take time. Accepting what happens when change occurs takes inner strength. Because acceptance is not giving up. Acceptance takes courage as well as faith and belief in yourself that you will be all right.

Affirmation

> **I release all tension and fear associated with change.**
> **I embrace change as a fresh, new beginning.**

Holistic Prescription

 Call to Action

Get excited about change as a fantastic chance to let go—of outdated things and ideas, people who no longer add to your value, and any extra baggage that no longer serves you—to accept the new normal as normal. Chant: "Out with the old, in with the new!"

 Mother Nature

Use these herbs: green tea for physical body regulation; clove for physical stimulation and positive energy attraction; and peppermint for enhanced healing, luck, love, and protection.

 Gemstones

Activate these gemstones: carnelian for strength, self-worth, and confidence; citrine for enhanced manifestation, personal will, and prosperity; and onyx for absorbing and transforming negative energy, plus increasing emotional and physical strength.

 Feng Shui

For optimal feng shui balance and harmony: Use earth elements for grounding; use green, blue, and teal colors to promote relaxation and calm; add wood elements to promote healing; add water elements and visit water sources such as oceans, rivers, and lakes for relaxation and letting go of the past, and to increase connection to the natural world.

39

ADAPT TO WHAT IS

Adapting to the new normal *is* the new normal. You never know what might come your way. Living in the present may look different than the past. Different than you imagined. Different than anyone thought it could. But, when you understand your life's circumstances, you realize that what is happening to you now is going to be your present life and you can adapt to it. When you take control, this is an active process, not a passive one.

Adapting does not mean that there is no confusion, pain, or suffering. It's natural to feel distress when something throws you off so much. At first, there will be a lot of chaos and uncertainty. This means the process is working.

You adapt when you recognize the need to make adjustments to become healthy and happy. Even in the worst of times, you can accept your circumstances and yet not be defined or limited by them, because you know the circumstances that you find yourself in are temporary. Stress can be blinding. Chilling out brings clarity.

You create your future, one day at a time, knowing that this is how real life presents itself. Even when times are tough. Even when you feel bad. Even when you are not sure about the "how." Remain flexible in the process toward your desired outcome, and, like water, you can adapt to change. Flowing... To stay sane on your path, you can focus on your flow.

Although sometimes life may feel more like a turbulent ocean, the river is gentle and curving, steady and accommodating as it moves to reach its ultimate destination. It is a model of how we can adapt and change in our careers, our relationships, and in anything else that comes our way. You can flow by doing things like:

- Staying active and moving forward
- Going around obstacles in your path
- Embracing opportunities to learn

Adaptation builds resilience. Building resilience means that you can bounce back from adversity more easily and quickly. Like palm trees in a storm, you can bend and sway to stay strong without losing the essence of who you are. Rather than becoming weak, you get stronger.

Affirmation

I adapt easily and effortlessly to change, creating beauty along the way.

Holistic Prescription

 Call to Action

With change and adaptation, be clear about the fact that you are expanding and growing.

 Mother Nature

Use these herbs: cedarwood for positive new beginnings; clove for physical stimulation and positive energy attraction; and lemon balm for physical restoration.

 Gemstones

Activate these gemstones: lapis for wisdom and serene awareness; rhodonite for emotional clearing from shock, trauma, and emotional wounds to achieve balance, self-love, and self-compassion; and jade for wisdom, peace, heart energy, and harmony.

 Feng Shui

For optimal feng shui balance and harmony: Use the fire color red to give you courage; include water elements to stay fluid and adaptable; use wood furnishings for growth and grounding.

40

CREATE PERSONAL STRATEGIES

Have you tried to do something the way "they" told you to do it and it still didn't work? Did you try it the way your cousin, friend, or coworker suggested and still, nothing? It may be time to be more creative. And more like you.

Success is not universal; how you define and achieve it is truly an individual experience. Similarly, a personal strategy is an effective way of doing what you do that is unique and personal to you. What works for someone else is not necessarily going to have the same impact for you and your life circumstances.

Uncover what your heart needs and what your soul values, and lead with that.

Progress doesn't always feel as great as you thought it would, especially when you are forging your own path. It's new. It's different. It's hard work! Knowing that ahead of time should save you some time, energy, and angst. And keep in mind…

We have to learn to be more patient with ourselves. And kind too. Sometimes, it's not three steps forward. Maybe it's five steps forward and two steps back. The whole is still the same. Don't focus on the two steps back. Focus on the three steps forward. And keep going.

When we focus on our dreams, we find that there are many steps to reach our goals. It's often not a giant leap but small, incremental, consistent efforts that help us reach the end. These small steps add up to something big, which makes the whole process a mighty one, not just the outcome.

So, what is your personal strategy? What works best for you when you do it? Take a deep breath and keep stepping. Take your time. And, yes, it's fine to keep making it up as you go along. In fact, let's encourage it—you are striving and adapting.

When you create personal strategies that work for you, you will know it. It feels seamless, even easy. It feels natural, not forced. You relax. And you get it done. You rise.

Affirmation

I actively engage in strategies that help me achieve my goals every day.

Holistic Prescription

 Call to Action

Remember that setbacks are not failures but a natural part of your learning curve.

 Mother Nature

Use these herbs and flowers to thrive: allspice for self-awareness, emotional healing, and luck; peppermint for enhanced healing, luck, love, and protection; and honeysuckle for beauty, personal power, and self-love.

 Gemstones

Activate these gemstones: peridot for positive energy, sunshine, and abundant blessings; black tourmaline for higher elevated thinking; and pyrite for transformative healing.

 Feng Shui

For optimal feng shui balance and harmony: Create open spaces; clear the clutter in your home and work spaces to inspire creativity; use metal furnishings and accessories for clarity, integrity, joy, and beauty; use water shapes and fountains to bring prosperity into your life; use fire elements like candles and red and orange colors for courage, inspiration, and dynamic energy.

41

ACT IN YOUR OWN BEST INTEREST

When you look out for yourself, you are not doing anything harmful to someone else. In other words, uplifting yourself doesn't mean hurting someone else. Chilling out doesn't hurt anybody, it helps us all.

You are your own ruler. It's your time. You decide what to do with your energy. Some people around you may not want you to act in your own best interest. Especially if you have not been doing it. They may even use that terrible "S" word to describe your actions: Selfish.

I know selfish people: colleagues, associates, and even family members. Classic narcissists. I am not talking about you being selfish like them. I am talking about you not being taken advantage of by people like them.

The curious thing is: Genuinely selfish people act in their own self-interest all the time and expect you to act in their best interest too. So, really, who's being selfish here?

Some of us find that we are very loyal to others, only to be disappointed when that level of caring is not reciprocated. Try this: Bring your energy inward. There you can find yourself. What you are really made of is hidden here. Pull yourself through. How? Know that *you* are what makes life worthwhile. You are worthy of that level of devotion, trust, and care. With unconditional self-love and prioritized self-care, you can approach life in a way that maybe you haven't thought of before.

Try putting yourself first. Know that helping others does not mean you have to sacrifice or harm yourself.

Acting in your own best interest includes making good financial decisions, maintaining excellent credit, using your time for personal growth activities, competent adulting, and being gentle with yourself when things don't work out the way you planned.

Can you do it? Will you? Not just for yourself, but for others. You may be surprised how good it feels.

Affirmation

In service to myself, my family, my community, and others, I prioritize my needs, acting with integrity and positive intention.

Holistic Prescription

 ### Call to Action

Make sure your support system is supporting your health, too, not just what you do for others.

 ### Mother Nature

Use these herbs and flowers: rose for increasing love vibrations, including self-love; jasmine for self-worth, beauty, and spiritual awareness; and rosemary for purified physical healing love.

 ### Gemstones

Activate these gemstones: black tourmaline for higher elevated thinking; fluorite for peace and increasing mental clarity; and spinel to realign your life with hope, gratitude, and appreciation.

 ### Feng Shui

For optimal feng shui balance and harmony: Add earth colors yellow, orange, and brown for self-care, boundaries, and stability; add metal colors white and gray for integrity, joy, beauty, and clarity; add water with circular shapes for prosperity and wisdom; add fire elements like red accents and bright lighting to increase confidence.

42

PREVENT SELF-SABOTAGE

Unconsciously, we self-sabotage:

- **When we focus on what we don't have:** A "lack" mentality can be crippling. The odds are too often stacked against us already, so any degree of self-sabotage makes absolutely no sense. Always envision prosperity and wealth.

- **When we procrastinate:** It is said that good things come to those who wait. But let's be honest with ourselves: Procrastination is not progress.

- **When we focus on the macro universe instead of our own everyday actions:** Does the weight of the world feel like it rests on your shoulders? You may think to yourself, "There's a lot going on." It's true. Something is always happening somewhere, historically and until the end of time.

- **When we take on more than we can reasonably handle:** We feel overwhelmed, believe that we never have enough time, feel tired every day, and wonder how we can break the cycle. We tend to look outward more than inward and become impatient more often and more quickly. We lose ourselves in the details of the day.

- **When we consistently put the needs of others ahead of our own:** Are you expected to take care of everyone? Some may say that this is your fault. We know it's deeper than that. It's not your fault that society often expects women to take care of everyone, or that your parents need assistance in their elder years, or that you weren't born wealthy, or that you overcommitted your time.... Your fault is not the same as your responsibility. It is your responsibility to make a good life for yourself.

Ultimately, you are responsible for you. Bring the focus back on yourself and your life.

Affirmation

I release behavior that does not serve me to engage in actions that uplift me.

Holistic Prescription

 Call to Action

Make a detailed plan to reclaim your time and energy spent taking care of others.

 Mother Nature

Use these herbs: skullcap for releasing and relinquishing control; thyme for spiritual awareness, plus healing with love and courage; and juniper berries for releasing negativity.

 Gemstones

Activate these gemstones: chrysoprase to help you recognize the grace and beauty in yourself; clear quartz for purification and inspiring creativity; and onyx for absorbing and transforming negative energy, plus increasing emotional and physical strength.

 Feng Shui

For optimal feng shui balance and harmony: Emphasize nature with plants; use water by cleansing in your bathtub for self-care, stability, knowledge, letting go, prosperity, and wealth; use yellow, orange, tan, blue, and green colors to help with establishing boundaries, growth, stability, and vitality; clear all clutter in your home and work spaces; avoid overcrowding furnishings that literally get in your way; surround yourself with uplifting artwork.

43

ESTABLISH BOUNDARIES

No one likes it when their boundaries are crossed. But first, are you sure that you clearly established and communicated your boundaries in the first place?

Boundaries generally come from what we learned about love as children. By chance, were you raised by narcissistic parents? If so, you probably have difficulties establishing boundaries. Were you raised to be a "good girl" and do as you're told? Then, you probably have difficulties establishing boundaries.

Give yourself permission to have boundaries. Honor them and expect those around you to honor them too. Or else…there will be consequences. Every relationship you have can be both a gift and a test. How do your loved ones and coworkers respond to your needs and desires?

Maybe your boundaries change. Maybe they are changing right now. That's to be expected. As you evolve, expect them to shift, especially with your most important relationships, including your parents, significant others, friends, and coworkers.

Some questions to ask yourself:

- What am I giving away too freely?
- Do they know my feelings and expectations?
- Are my actions being reciprocated?
- Am I getting what I need from this relationship?

If you find that your boundaries are not being respected, it's never too late to make a change. Setting boundaries is the ultimate form of self-care, self-love, and self-respect. Being wishy-washy is no state to be in, so make a decision and stick to it. You will be thankful that you did.

Affirmation

I establish and enforce my personal boundaries, and if they are crossed, I act immediately.

Holistic Prescription

 Call to Action

Feel free to tell others, "Hold on, things are different now."

 Mother Nature

Use these herbs and flowers: allspice for self-awareness, emotional healing, and luck; honeysuckle for beauty, personal power, and self-love; and peppermint for enhanced healing, luck, love, and protection.

 Gemstones

Activate these gemstones: apatite for willpower and strength through love; labradorite for intuition and to protect your aura; and garnet for chi stimulation and to remove emotional blockages in the body.

 Feng Shui

For optimal feng shui balance and harmony: Add metal colors white and gray for increased clarity and precision; add water elements with blue water colors for connection and wisdom, plus increased intuition.

44

REMOVE OBSTACLES

Do you know that being agitated, stressed out, anxious, and afraid blocks your blessings?

Most of us assume that success makes us happy. But, no, it's actually the other way around: Happiness makes you successful. So, what's the quickest path to happiness? Health and happiness can both be achieved by chilling out.

By identifying the barriers to your health and happiness, you can remove them, one by one, to begin to relax, let go, and heal. Notice that you are not "overcoming" obstacles. Instead of going through them—oftentimes a miserable, long, arduous process—let's just kick obstacles to the curb. Let's remove obstacles completely.

When a challenge comes your way, your first thought might be to shrink and back away. But if you see challenges as opportunities for special rewards, maybe they're yours to receive. It's not too much; it's the perfect thing for you right now. It's a call to action to improve the quality of your life.

Your tight grip on what used to be has been a big barrier to you living a full life. Laughing, loving, by yourself, with friends and family…are in your present and future. Holding onto the past is unnecessary, unhelpful, and unhealthy.

Removing obstacles may take some time. No need for insecurity or impatience when things aren't going the way you want them to. Just relax. Just wait. Keep going and don't give up. You'll see.

You have everything you need to meet challenges and succeed. What if you fail? What if you don't? What if, what if…enough of this type of hypothetical worrying. Perhaps, you need a boost of confidence or a little nudge to make the big leap. Here it is—do it!

Expect the desired outcome. By putting in the work and understanding the process, you will see that it is not just attainable; it's pretty much inevitable. How did the obstacle get there? Doesn't matter. Remove it.

Be inevitable. Stay invincible. Your big achievement awaits…

Affirmation

I claim victory over any obstacles to my health, happiness, and success.

Holistic Prescription

 Call to Action

Learn to approach obstacles without fear by relying on your strengths and your resilience.

 Mother Nature

Use these herbs and flowers: honeysuckle for beauty, personal power, and self-love; clove for physical stimulation and positive energy attraction; and peppermint for enhanced healing, luck, love, and protection.

 Gemstones

Activate these gemstones: citrine for enhanced manifestation, personal will, and prosperity; blue agate for patience, peace, hope, and positive thinking; and howlite for remaining true to yourself and to soothe emotions.

 Feng Shui

For optimal feng shui balance and harmony: Add fire colors red and orange for confidence, strength, and courage; add wood colors green and blue for vitality; add earth elements like ceramics and stone for growth and healing.

45

LET IT GO, FOR REAL

Where do you go from here? It's a good question…and one that only you can answer. The only way, really, is forward—not ruminating about the past, carrying regret, or worrying about what may or may not happen.

Dreaming about the good times you used to have? What about painful memories? Pain often has a stronger physical response and impact on our memories than pleasure. Also, many of us are taught that going back to our past trauma is useful, even therapeutic. Well, not for everybody. Maybe it's not for you.

You don't have to constantly relive a painful past experience. Why let go of the past? Because when you recall it, your body, mind, and spirit remember it (again!) and experience it in the present, even though it's firmly rooted in the past.

It's amazing how much easier it can seem to look back at what used to be, rather than look forward to an unknown future. Living in the past, even when it hurts, seems comfortable and secure. But… don't do it. If you stay in the past, whether good or bad, you get stuck there. Breaking any and all unproductive feedback loops is a necessary step to make space for real progress. Right now.

Contrary to popular belief, the past does *not* predict the present or the future. The past is the past. Period. Full stop. That's it. The present and future? Well, that's really up to you.

Nothing is going to change if you keep holding onto history. Now is the time to live. We move forward by not getting stuck on what happened or what was. What is and what will be are truly up to you.

You make your reality right here, right now, and what happened before matters less and less each time you focus on your wonderful present and your bright future.

Know that the present and the future have good things waiting for you. Then, you can move forward with intention, clarity, and promise. The future is bright! More happy times are here, waiting for you. You just have to focus on today.

Affirmation

I release the past right now and live today for myself, my family, and my community.

Holistic Prescription

Call to Action

When you find yourself thinking about the past, *stop*. Refocus on this moment right now, your current projects, friends, and activities. Embrace hope by remembering to be grateful.

Mother Nature

Use these herbs: skullcap for releasing and relinquishing control; thyme for spiritual awareness, plus healing with love and courage; and juniper berries for releasing negativity.

Gemstones

Activate these gemstones: jade for wisdom, peace, heart energy, and harmony; aventurine to bring joy, acceptance, and well-being; and spinel to realign your life with hope, gratitude, and appreciation.

Feng Shui

For optimal feng shui balance and harmony: Reduce all clutter, especially in corners and on flat surfaces to physically let go of things that no longer serve you; add a small water fountain to help things flow onward and move on; ground yourself with earth elements like stones and clay planters.

46

OVERCOME BLIND SPOTS

Whoa, didn't see that coming! What is it about our blind spots that makes us so vulnerable and super reactive? Maybe it's because we don't know what they are…we don't see them. By not being aware of our blind spots, we lose our power and experience loss.

Like a blind spot in a car, blind spots in our lives are just there. Yet even though we know that we have a blind spot in the car, we still choose to drive. So, no, you are not deficient. We all have blind spots hidden in our psyches, yet we still succeed.

Many of us are fighting progress without realizing it. We do it because we don't always understand what progress looks like. But what can we really see anyway? We are blind to most happenings in our lives. Our minds may be limited by personal experience, but, ladies, let's expand our thinking. If we use our *third eye* (our intuitive inherent spiritual guidance) to see, we see so much more.

As we are learning more about flying blind through life, we can ask ourselves, "Do we always have to 'see' our greatness first to become great?" The answer is an obvious "no." Your destiny may look nothing like what you pictured for yourself, but that doesn't make a wonderful life less wonderful.

Know that there are such good things waiting for your future self, even if you don't see them right now. This is what it means to *walk in faith*. We don't have to be limited by our imaginations. What you can "see" is only a very small part of the Universe and your life path. Like gravity, you don't have to see it to believe it.

To help you identify your blind spots, think about these questions:

- What behaviors in others have surprised you the most?
- What has hurt you the most?
- When you've misjudged someone's character, who was it, and what happened?

Just like driving a car, blind spots won't stop you. You can still get to your destination.

Affirmation

I walk in faith knowing that I do not need to totally "see" my process to be successful.

Holistic Prescription

 Call to Action
Know that your blind spots exist, and identify what they are. To overcome your blind spots, use more objective measures to supplement your own analysis.

 Mother Nature
Use these herbs: allspice for self-awareness, emotional healing, and luck; peppermint for enhanced healing, luck, love, and protection; and thyme for spiritual awareness, plus healing with love and courage.

 Gemstones
Activate these gemstones: black tourmaline for higher elevated thinking; fluorite for peace and increasing mental clarity; and sodalite for getting in tune with your intuition and higher consciousness.

 Feng Shui
For optimal feng shui balance and harmony: Add metal colors white and gray for increased clarity and precision; add water elements with blue water colors for connection and wisdom, plus increased intuition.

47

EXPAND YOUR MIND

Are you afraid to trust again? To take risks? To go for it? That "fear of the unknown" kind of energy (lack of wholeness, self-acceptance, and confidence, plus holding onto the past) makes it difficult to find what you want the most. Expanding your mind will challenge you to answer questions about who and what you think you are; when we learn more about ourselves, we learn to be better. Then, we can go inward and beyond what we thought we were capable of—deeper, expanding, growing, learning…

For most of us, expanding the mind means going above and beyond self-help activities like reading and therapy. These activities are extremely helpful, but what really elevates understanding and helps you gain clarity is a spiritual practice—specifically, a ritual of prayer, meditation, or other exercise rooted in higher understanding. We have to go to the soul level.

Your soul wants you to be healthy and happy. Your soul can rescue you from yourself. What is the value of having this wise inner voice that can show you the way when you make a habit of ignoring it? Let's change this right away by expanding what we think and believe is possible.

We are constantly bombarded by information, sometimes confusing *mis*information. The mind can be manipulated by external stimuli and will be utterly directionless without the soul. The soul intuitively tells your mind what to do. Expanding your mind must include connection to your soul to figure out where to go.

Although your soul cannot be manipulated and tricked, it can be overshadowed by a mind that constantly provides noise—for example, a voice that self-criticizes or consistently tells your body to keep repeating unhealthy habits, never mind the costs.

There is a solution. Nurture your soul, engage your spirit, and when it speaks, don't just listen—act. Your highest good is waiting for you to claim it.

Affirmation

I expand how I think, what I believe and understand to empower myself, my family, and my community.

Holistic Prescription

 Call to Action

Reframe challenges as opportunities to expand your way of problem-solving and experiencing life.

 Mother Nature

Use these herbs and flowers: cedarwood for positive new beginnings; gardenia for expansive healing and peaceful self-love; and bay leaves for spiritual enhancement and protection.

 Gemstones

Activate these gemstones: citrine for enhanced manifestation, personal will, and prosperity; carnelian for strength, self-worth, and confidence; and black tourmaline for higher elevated thinking.

 Feng Shui

For optimal feng shui balance and harmony: Add metal elements like white, gray, and gold/silver/copper metallic colors to improve clarity and integrity; add wood furnishings and green and blue colors for growth, flexibility, and trust; add fire elements, particularly scented candles, to increase inspiration, dynamic energy, confidence, and vitality.

48

SLOW DOWN TO MOVE FORWARD

When you feel overwhelmed, tired, and need a break—take the break. Contrary to what others might think, a break is a step forward, not a step back or even a pause.

You can achieve a lot by doing very little.

With the fast pace of the world today, it's easy to forget to sit down and just breathe. When we take a break, we connect with the deeper part of our subconscious mind that can create our desires more deeply and completely. And it works fast! We are breaking through by breaking free, taking time away from the thing that we are struggling with. This is how we overcome barriers and get ahead.

Try to be still for five minutes today. Notice how that feels. If your mind wanders, that's okay. What were you thinking? Where did you go?

Now, instead of allowing your mind to wander, picture something you want badly in your life right now. Imagine having it and enjoying it. This should feel pretty good!

To make the vision of what you want in your life a reality for yourself, you can create space by first taking the time to see it. Slowing…down… to get the big picture. By affirming your desires first with your time, then with your mind, you can begin to manifest it in real time. To a casual observer, this important activity looks like "doing not very much."

Creative visualization and daydreams serve a purpose. But first, you need to create space for it. Every day.

Affirmation

For at least five minutes today, I will slow down to focus on myself and my breathing, and to dream my dreams.

Holistic Prescription

 Call to Action

Avoid multitasking. Keep your intentions focused on what is right in front of you to find peace and stability in your everyday tasks.

 Mother Nature

Use these herbs and flowers: chamomile for calming relaxation; lavender for peaceful relaxation and restorative rest; and gardenia for expansive healing and peaceful self-love.

 Gemstones

Activate these gemstones: fluorite for peace and increasing mental clarity; smoky quartz for grounding and balance; and larimar for stillness, calm, and chilling vibes.

 Feng Shui

For optimal feng shui balance and harmony: Add earth elements like pottery and stones for grounding, stability, and self-care; use metal elements like mirrors, artwork, lights, and other objects of interest that cause people to pause and slow down; add fire elements with candles and incense that includes frankincense, pine, sage, and sandalwood; visit the sea to relax, release, and let go.

49

GAIN CLARITY

Most women I know want to be successful. I bet you do too. Of course, deliberate action is required to achieve set goals. Deliberate action requires clarity—in work, business, and life.

Are you clear about what you want? Are you certain regarding what is needed to get there? Do you picture it, every detail and nuance, in your vision and mind's eye? "Focus on your dreams" means literal focus. Driven. Intense. Deliberate. Unrelenting. Focus.

Maybe you're a multitasker, doing two or three things at once. Distracted by social media, you may find yourself going down a rabbit hole, losing hours at a time. *Stop It.* Even if you could do everything all at once, you shouldn't. Even if you can find something of value in social media, social media is not about you. Our brains, bodies, and spirits are incredible, yet we can maximize our personal power only when we focus on one thing at a time.

Focus on yourself, maybe for the first time. You are many things to many people. That doesn't mean you have to constantly do multiple tasks at once with divided intention and attention.

Most of us want a good, quality life. Maybe you are starting to realize that you can add power to your vision. Try your best to be clear, precise, and imperfectly perfect. If your vision is fuzzy and nonspecific, your achievements toward that goal are likely to be the same. Choose one task to complete in one time frame.

Live your life like the ultimate movie. It's your movie, your life. Add beauty to your clarification process, because beauty makes all things possible, bright, and shiny. Some tasks are a work in progress (like your life journey!) while other tasks need to get done right now. Know, too, that there are often many small steps toward achieving big goals.

Affirmation

Holistic Prescription

 Call to Action

With clarity, choose your tasks, differentiating between immediate ones and those pesky distractions that do not require your energy right now.

 Mother Nature

Use these herbs: black cohosh for hormone regulation; clove for physical stimulation and positive energy attraction; and passionflower to reduce restlessness, anxiety, and insomnia.

 Gemstones

Activate these gemstones: alexandrite for identifying and developing joy within yourself, and for wisdom and serene awareness; and labradorite for intuition and to protect your aura.

 Feng Shui

For optimal feng shui balance and harmony: Add metal colors white and gray for integrity, joy, beauty, and clarity; add water with circular shapes for prosperity and wisdom.

50

BE MORE THAN YOUR FEELINGS

On this beautiful journey of healing and self-discovery, we are coming to understand what many of us already know: Starting, stopping, and starting over again is part of our process. On the path to constantly creating and recreating ourselves, we realize that change is inevitable and constant. The same is true of our feelings.

Your feelings are valid, and you are worthy. Yet you can be even more. You can be more than your feelings. Because what you feel today is not necessarily how you will feel in an hour, a day, a week, a year…you are so much more than these temporary, sometimes fleeting emotional sensations.

Don't disconnect from who you are. Don't ignore how you feel and what you are experiencing. And don't reduce yourself to just these feelings alone. Don't doubt what you are, who you are becoming, and how you are expanding. And know that this, too, shall pass. Even when a feeling is getting intense, full of doom and gloom, it will eventually move on and disappear. It goes away. When you realize that this feel-bad moment is fleeting, you can relax and rest assured that tomorrow is a new day.

Consider, too, that it's not always about you. Sometimes when people say thoughtless, insensitive things to us or do mean things, we take it personally, whether or not we even know them. We often allow faceless people to hurt us when they don't even know us and we certainly do not know them. This speaks volumes about who they are and less about us. We are more than our feelings. We don't have to internalize these unproductive thoughts and feelings. If they get through, let them roll downhill and away. Or vaporize into thin air, like smoke. Maintain yourself in peace, knowing that you live for yourself, not for other people.

When you keep it positive, keep it light, keep it simple, and stay divine, your positive growth is pretty much guaranteed.

Affirmation

I use my feelings to show me areas of potential growth and improvement.

Holistic Prescription

 Call to Action

Resist the urge to stay in your feelings for too long; let them pass.

 Mother Nature

Use these herbs: thyme for spiritual awareness, plus healing with love and courage; rosemary for purified physical healing love; and cinnamon for grounding and balancing energy.

 Gemstones

Activate these gemstones: jade for wisdom, peace, heart energy, and harmony; tiger's eye for increasing confidence while releasing fear and anxiety; and pyrite for transformative healing.

 Feng Shui

For optimal feng shui balance and harmony: Clear all clutter; use earth elements like terra-cotta pots and plants for grounding, self-care, and boundaries; use water elements like circular shapes and the water color dark blue to promote deep wisdom; use metal accents for integrity.

51

FIND YOUR INNER VOICE

Uh oh, things are definitely not going as planned. Now what? Try this: Close your eyes. Go inward. Listen to your inner voice, your intuition. Don't "try" to listen. Just listen. In stillness, in peace, and in wisdom. Your soul voice is trying to tell you something. Hear it. Believe it. Because your inner voice knows. While you think about all the potential solutions, it already has the answers. It's there to help you. To make sure that you know that you are never alone. Instead of using choice and personal will to push your way along a path that may or may not be best for you, find and use the innate wisdom of your inner voice to inform your next steps.

When did you decide to stop listening to your inner voice and just do what you want to do, when you want to do it? Maybe it's because you realized that you could. But should you? There is a reason to every season. Universal law and karma are real. Sure, we have the capacity to choose our actions and can use it, too, but many of us fail to realize that we lose something big when we ignore our inner voice. It knows what you do not, so, most of the time, we don't even realize how much we've been losing!

While we were failing to listen to our inner voices, we were also failing to chill out. Your inner voice tells you when to chill. Are you listening? Chilling out is the ultimate in relaxation. Relaxation includes powerful moments of self-exploration, self-awareness, and self-discovery. The link between finding your inner voice and chilling out is undeniable; they are part of the same.

Whatever is coming, let it come. You are prepared to handle whatever comes your way.

Affirmation

I am fortified when I channel the wisdom of my inner voice; I know it, feel it, and live this truth.

Holistic Prescription

 Call to Action

Use relaxation tactics like meditation, being in nature, solitude, and your spiritual practice to help you find and listen to your inner voice.

 Mother Nature

Use these herbs: peppermint for enhanced healing, luck, love, and protection; sage for spiritual purification and new positive beginnings; and juniper berries for releasing negativity.

 Gemstones

Activate these gemstones: tiger's eye for increasing confidence while releasing fear and anxiety; sodalite for getting in tune with your intuition and higher consciousness; and aventurine for nurturing yourself, bringing joy, and a positive attitude.

 Feng Shui

For optimal feng shui balance and harmony: Clear all clutter; use water elements like circular tables and shapes to increase connection; meditate on a floor cushion for grounding using earth colors yellow, brown, and tan; use wood elements like plants for spiritual nourishment.

52

CUT THROUGH THE NOISE

Drama scatters our energy and clouds our judgment. Some emergencies are not actual emergencies and others are not our responsibility. Some issues are simply not ours to take on. When you are initially confronted with chaotic energy and Other People's Problems (OPPs), your choices become…less clear. The world is a huge place, and we're not always in a position to do something about OPPs right now. Maybe not later, either. Like clearing clutter on a desk or in a corner, making space makes all the difference. When you think about it this way, reducing the unnecessary and unwanted background noise is the clearest way to focus on yourself in the present.

If we are all busy doing our own thing *and* we engage people with competing agendas, we inevitably end up with a noisy mess, lack of productivity, miscommunication, and lack of unity. A lot of people talking and competing for attention is loud, jarring, and off-putting. Instead of allowing it to continue, you can remove all the voices except one or two that specifically pertain to you and your purpose. In this space, you can find both peace and focus.

Like doing an online search, you have to be specific to target what you want and ignore the rest; you don't need the entire world wide web, just a small sliver of it to use for your enlightenment. Concentrating on what you are doing right now is so important, because it is what you are shifting into both independently and with those around you: how you live your personal life and what the world will look like.

Blocking competition, noise, and conflict increases personal success, self-development, and unity of thought and action, a symphony of like-mindedness. Like stars, our bright lights can shine in the sky together. Like a choir, our voices can harmonize.

Affirmation

> **I block out noisy distractions, finding peace and focus to achieve my dreams.**

Holistic Prescription

 Call to Action

Make a pledge not to gossip, because negative energy focusing on other people creates noise. Instead, focus on yourself and what you are doing with your life.

 Mother Nature

Use these herbs and flowers: yarrow for protecting and raising the frequency of love vibrations; honeysuckle for beauty, personal power, and self-love; and thyme for spiritual awareness, plus healing with love and courage.

 Gemstones

Activate these gemstones: blue agate for patience, peace, hope, and positive thinking; carnelian for strength, self-worth, and confidence; and turquoise for health and inner calm.

 Feng Shui

For optimal feng shui balance and harmony: Clear all clutter; add a water fountain for calm, relaxation, and peaceful focus; add wood elements with plants and flowers for healing, growth, and trust.

53

OVERCOME THE HEARTBREAK

Some of us love to be in love. We lose ourselves in the state and get carried away on cloud nine like an addict. Our strength and willpower come from love. Rather than lose yourself in love, let it take you higher. Wrap yourself in love. Your love. For yourself. For you. And then, for others too.

When you are a caring and giving person, it's easy to get caught up putting everyone else's needs first. But…this is about you getting your mojo back. No longer lost in love, reclaim yourself. It's your heart. *Yours.* Maybe you gave your good stuff away to your lover, your partner, the person you thought was your soul mate. Maybe you tend to give your good stuff away to causes you care about, your job, your furry friends, and your family. But, do you also give it to yourself?

It is difficult to see at the time, but it is a fact: We can get past the feeling of being heartbroken. When you can reactivate your *anahata*, the heart chakra, you can heal it, reinforce its protective qualities, and keep it vibrating at a high frequency. Just remember, don't give it all away.

You will find the key to healthy, loving relationships. And overcoming heartbreak. It's there. Things are uncertain after your heart is broken, but one thing you should know for sure is that touch and physical contact will help. For some of us, the lack of physical intimacy after regularly having that kind of closeness is almost unbearable. Before you rush into anything foolish, know that the best intimacy comes from a place of pure love. This may be a hug from your mother or your best friend, not sex with a stranger.

Our soul mates are sometimes there to teach us the karmic lessons that we need to learn, not just provide fun and good times. In your journey, you can process your wounds and provide love to others at the same time. So, continue to give love and give it freely. It *will* come back to you.

Affirmation

I reclaim my self and my love energy every day, in all ways.

Holistic Prescription

 Call to Action

Resist the urge to withdraw love and affection when experiencing a heartbreak. Feel your feelings and move past the grief by having faith in love—continue to explore all types of love.

 Mother Nature

Use these herbs and flowers: rose for increasing love vibrations, including self-love; yarrow for protecting and raising the frequency of love vibrations; and jasmine for self-worth, beauty, and spiritual awareness.

 Gemstones

Activate these gemstones: rose quartz for gentle self-love and emotional healing by releasing resentments; rhodonite for stimulating, clearing, and activating the heart; and lepidolite for attracting love, hope, and light, plus change acceptance.

 Feng Shui

For optimal feng shui balance and harmony: Surround yourself with loving energy, such as beautiful artwork, mirrors, and candles; add wood with flowers; clear clutter and anything that reminds you of your heartache; add earth elements with soft and natural textures, for comfort and grounding; add pink and yellow for self-love (fire and earth elements); add metal accents for joy and beauty.

54

UNPLUG TO UNWIND

Do you ever catch yourself reminiscing about the old days when you didn't receive instant notifications on your cell phone and folks at work and home didn't expect instant replies to their emails and texts? Or maybe you were born during the decades with this technology already in place. Maybe you only fantasize about existing in a tech-free world. If only.

You don't have to change the whole world to change your life. Most people will receive great benefits from unplugging from technology, even just a little bit, like an hour or two, or overnight. When you turn off all the technology, you are creating a tech-free zone, a space for you to just be. You can exist with no worries, no false alarms, and no drama. In other words, you will find peace.

The radioactive waves and blue-light energy emitted from your cell phone are not just dangerous to your health. They also prevent you from resting appropriately, making it more difficult to chill out when they are in constant use.

Maybe you've tried to unplug before and couldn't do it for very long. If it's new for you, be patient with yourself. Keep trying. Unplugging may seem extreme, like being at a silent retreat or going to a nudist camp. But, no, this is not an extreme act, just one coming from self-love, self-care, and self-preservation. By unplugging, you can focus on yourself, the here and now, and gain clarity without distraction. The world is still spinning; you are just not reacting to everything that is going on at the same time in this moment.

What do you do when you unplug? Nothing. That's the point! It's unnatural to be on call all the time. It's natural to chill out. On your own terms, the space to be you is priceless.

Affirmation

> **I embrace my freedom by unplugging from technology on a regular basis.**

Holistic Prescription

 Call to Action

Understand FOMO as a real phenomenon that social media and advertisers exploit to get you to engage with them constantly and consistently. Reject the Fear of Missing Out!

 Mother Nature

Use these herbs: chamomile for calming relaxation; passionflower to reduce restlessness, anxiety, and insomnia; and parsley for detoxification.

 Gemstones

Activate these gemstones: alexandrite for identifying and developing joy within yourself; peridot for positive energy, sunshine, and abundant blessings; and fluorite for dispelling negative energy and stabilizing emotions.

 Feng Shui

For optimal feng shui balance and harmony: Clear clutter; remove technology (TVs, radios, computers) from your bedroom; add lots of wood elements like plants and flowers to enhance self-care and healing; add circular patterns to maintain connectedness to people, not things.

55

RELEASE GRIEF

There is a saying that you need to know the darkness to know the light. Releasing grief works like this too. Living in grief is like being in the dark. Releasing grief brings you into the light.

Love is the thing that connects us all. While you are conscious and developing your inner self, remember to always include love. Just know that it won't always be sunshine and rainbows; love is pain too. This is what it means to be a flesh-and-spirit adult human being with choices and experiences.

When something happens that we don't like, we often feel bad. We can choose to stay feeling bad and wallow in grief about what was, or we can see the good in what was just released. Ruminating about horrible things that make you sad is dysfunctional and dangerous. When grief takes over, it smashes you down, like a 1,000-pound gorilla on your chest.

Your day-to-day is much harder when you feel sad. Prioritizing self-care and therapy can help you work through grief. But first, you must want more for yourself. You must be willing to disconnect. Wanting more helps you choose light. Choose love. Choose freedom. Choose life. When you choose, the Universe works with you. Because you give it something uplifting to work with, your spirit works with you. It *will* help you. Carry you. Bring joy back into your life.

Grief is thick and intense energy. Maybe you don't want to release it. Maybe you want to be mad, angry, sad, and miserable. Maybe you've gotten used to it or you're stuck. That's when it's time to disconnect.

Remember that it's okay to be stuck at first, but you deserve so much more. So, work to get free. When you release negative energy, you make space to replace it with something great. You also break free from the hold that the past has on you. Only you can sever this thick and heavy cord that binds.

Affirmation

I free myself from misery and grief because my life is filled with joyful possibilities.

Holistic Prescription

 Call to Action

Be honest with yourself: Think of what will make you healthy and whole again. Focus on that. Release and replace. Also, be honest about what you are doing and whether it is working for you. If not, do not hesitate to seek help.

 Mother Nature

Use these plants: thyme for spiritual awareness, plus healing with love and courage; cedarwood for positive new beginnings; and lime to promote healing that prioritizes love.

 Gemstones

Activate these gemstones: moss agate for increased immune functioning, happiness, and overall balance; aventurine to bring joy, acceptance, and well-being; and aquamarine to clear the mind and connect to higher health and well-being.

 Feng Shui

For optimal feng shui balance and harmony: Remove all clutter and anything that reminds you of your grief; add a small water fountain to help things flow onward and move on; add wood elements, such as plants and flowers, especially peace lilies and orchids; use white, green, and blue colors for grounding, healing, and stillness; burn sage and frankincense to release using a powerful fire element.

56

GIVE LOVE FREELY

Love is boundless. You will always have enough. To give. To receive. Love is respect. Love is trust. It's also admiration. And, of course, affection. We feel this way about ourselves and others. Love expresses itself in a myriad of magnificent ways.

Loving yourself can be tricky stuff. Being nice to yourself, no matter what, can be complicated business. Even though it may be hard sometimes, it's necessary. Self-love and self-acceptance are the greatest gifts we can give ourselves, right now and forever until the end of time. It is the foundation of our capacity to give love. With it, you can love freely, without fear.

Love, like other important aspects of life, is a spiritual game. Like most games, they're more fun when you don't overanalyze. Lighten up! Instead of trying to figure it out, enjoy playing. Sometimes you'll win. Sometimes you may lose. However, even your loss is better than sitting on the sidelines wondering "What if?" You definitely won't get anything if you don't try.

The energy we have is so precious. It's precious and powerful. There are no limits to how you can love yourself and others. When you love yourself, your world opens up and attracts even more love. So why wait? You don't have to wait for love. It's all right there inside you. Turn it on.

Stingy love is almost like not loving at all. Same with fearful love. And shameful love. Our partners, family members, friends, employees, pets, and plants all need our love and attention to thrive. Can you give it to them?

Not everyone deserves what we have to offer, and not everyone can give what we give. Give love without expecting the exact same in return. Give only what you are comfortable giving.

Real love, no regrets. While you are at it, don't forget to give love and affection to yourself freely too.

Affirmation

I am love. I give and receive love freely.

Holistic Prescription

 Call to Action

Give it all today, 100 percent love. See how you feel and how others react.

 Mother Nature

Use these herbs and flowers: rose for increasing love vibrations, including self-love; yarrow for protecting and raising the frequency of love vibrations; and gardenia for expansive healing and peaceful self-love.

 Gemstones

Activate these gemstones: rose quartz for warm, caring, gentle self-love and emotional healing by releasing resentments; jade for wisdom, peace, heart energy, and harmony; and malachite for purification and attracting love by opening the heart.

 Feng Shui

For optimal feng shui balance and harmony: Surround yourself with loving energy, such as beautiful artwork, mirrors, and candles; add wood with flowers; clear all clutter in your home; bring more feminine (yin) elements into your work space and home, especially your bedroom—for example, include metal elements with curvy furniture and earth elements with soft and natural textures and pastel colors like pink and yellow; add metal accents for joy and beauty; add fire elements for passion and inspiration including orange and red colors.

57

INCREASE COMPASSION

Your inner child needs compassion. She needs to be seen, loved, and validated. She needs you to handle your business and have fun too. She needs her feelings to be acknowledged. Your healing journey requires compassion. Have you ever looked in the mirror and told yourself that you need "something" today? Maybe what you really need is a hug. In the absence of compassion, we can lose what matters most—ourselves. Worrying robs so much time and energy. Being kind to yourself is the beginning of the end of worry.

You give compassionate care to the dog, the cat, your friends, your neighbors; that's great. You are clearly a person who cares. Just make sure to hold onto some of that for yourself too. How do you keep from giving it all away? With self-compassion.

Self-compassion means being kind to yourself, avoiding self-criticism and negative self-talk. It is patience with your imperfections. It is letting go of temporary disappointments to get on with your day. This is how compassion enhances adaptation. With understanding and acceptance of difficult circumstances, we are empowered to learn more and make positive changes that guide our journey.

How can you be compassionate with your time and responsibilities? Try these suggestions:

- Realize that you can't be everywhere and everything for everybody.
- Practice saying "no."
- If you keep a schedule, don't forget to include your "me" time.

Do you know what also helps? Meditation, of course. Meditation helps nurture the inner child with a caring, knowledgeable inner voice. It's gentle, kind, and nurturing.

Affirmation

> **I honor myself and my daily needs with gentle love and kindness.**

Holistic Prescription

 Call to Action

Convert a quiet corner into a small meditation and prayer area as your personal, sacred safe space.

 Mother Nature

Use these herbs and flowers: rose for increasing love vibrations, including self-love and self-compassion; allspice for self-awareness, emotional healing, and luck; and yarrow for protecting and raising the frequency of love vibrations.

 Gemstones

Activate these gemstones: rhodochrosite for emotional healing from childhood trauma and reclaiming self; lepidolite for attracting love, hope, and light, plus change acceptance; and aventurine for nurturing yourself, bringing joy, and a positive attitude.

 Feng Shui

For optimal feng shui balance and harmony: Clear the clutter in your home; add earth elements and use earth colors yellow and beige for self-care, boundaries, and stability; add the water color blue to increase connection and release old wounds; add wood elements like the color green to increase trust and kindness.

58

BALANCE EMOTIONS

Joy. Pleasure. Grief. Pain. It feels so good to feel good and so bad to feel bad. Emotions are not bad. Most people only like to feel good, but it's all about the balance. Yin and yang. Most of our time is spent in the middle, the in-between.

When you are unbalanced, anything or anyone can easily set you off. Poor service at a restaurant, an insulting comment from a colleague at work, the loss of a loved one… Your heart pounds, you feel like screaming, you're so frustrated, and wham! You're all messed up. Stuff happens. The stuff is not "small" or "big." Something can affect you a lot or a little. We don't all react the same way. And how you react (or not) can have cumulative effects.

When you feel sadness, worry, fear, and anxiety, it can be very challenging to get "right" again. Know thyself. When you know yourself, you know your triggers so that you are not led by them. You can respond to life's happenings—without breaking down.

When you are upset, how do you soothe yourself? What brings you immediate comfort? Who helps you achieve and maintain your peace?

A balanced state is a naturally neutral state. Balancing your emotions… Being emotionally steady means understanding that you can't predict the events of your days and the feelings that these events will produce. When you first begin, you must try to balance your emotions. When you find a technique or process that helps you balance your emotions, you must practice it. Your process must be known to you and well rehearsed. Deep breathing. Thoughtful introspection. Meditation. Your own personal process to release intense emotions and inner torment is a deliberate one. Getting back to comfort and confidence…yes, that's more like it.

When your balancing process is well established, it can be available to you when you need it. Eventually, you won't have to make as much effort because the process will be so familiar that it becomes second nature.

Affirmation

I balance my emotions knowing that they are good for me and a healthy part of who I am.

Holistic Prescription

 Call to Action
Have a balancing ritual, such as drinking hot tea, taking a bath, or talking to a friend.

 Mother Nature
Use these herbs: allspice for self-awareness, emotional healing, and luck; sage for spiritual purification and new positive beginnings; and cinnamon for grounding and balancing energy.

 Gemstones
Activate these gemstones: malachite for transformation, clearing, balancing, soothing turbulent emotions, and calming rage; unakite for removing negativity and balancing emotions; and moss agate for increased immune functioning, happiness, and overall balance.

 Feng Shui
For optimal feng shui balance and harmony: Use earth colors beige, tan, and yellow to promote balance and calm; add wood furnishings and the color green to promote healing; add water elements like the sound of ocean waves for relaxation.

59

EXPRESS YOURSELF

Self-expression is the ultimate way to exist and show the world who you are. It's also the perfect opportunity to express a more chilled-out persona. What that means is up to you. When done correctly, or even when it's done incorrectly, if it's authentic, it's true and wonderful. Self-expression is:

- Serious
- Committed
- Ever-evolving
- Diverse
- Layered
- Distinct
- Courageous
- Fresh
- Powerful

What makes complex women want to keep things simple? Limited self-expression often comes from value-driven fear. Maybe you've been playing it safe. Do you take risks or are you more conservative? Do you like to be noticed or prefer to blend in the background?

Maybe your outer you does not reflect your inner you at all. If you can express yourself in any and all ways possible, consider what your life looks and feels like with different:

- Clothes
- Hairstyles
- Work
- Friends
- Homes
- Hobbies
- Tattoos
- Piercings
- Food

Because we are all affected differently by life's happenings, how we heal is a form of self-expression too. Because your wounds were inflicted and internalized in your own unique way, your healing journeys will take many forms too. Don't be afraid to express the many parts of you: healed, healing, and unhealed.

Affirmation

I am fearless in my self-expression and excited to try new things.

Holistic Prescription

 Call to Action

Gather the courage to express your true self. What does it look like?

 Mother Nature

Use these herbs and flowers: allspice for self-awareness, emotional healing, and luck; jasmine for self-worth, beauty, and spiritual awareness; and honeysuckle for beauty, personal power, and self-love.

 Gemstones

Activate these gemstones: labradorite for intuition and to protect your aura; aventurine to bring joy, acceptance, and well-being; and kyanite for maximizing your full potential and uplifting self-expression.

 Feng Shui

For optimal feng shui balance and harmony: Use all five elements (water, wood, earth, metal, fire), but in your own unique way; use metal frames and furnishings for joy and beauty; use water colors and fountains for flowing momentum and depth in your self-expression; use lots of plants for wood; and use the colors, red, pink, and bright orange to stimulate interest and courage.

60

GO NEXT-LEVEL

There's what you think you can do, and then there's what you can do. Know that what you think you can do is usually far less than your actual capacity. Too often we underestimate ourselves. We can do way more than we think, and understanding this reality can help us move farther, faster. Let's set the bar higher.

Sometimes we have to ask ourselves, "Are you comfortable or stagnant? Are you being content or complacent? Are you being realistic or settling?" It's time to go next-level.

There's one major reason that people don't reach their full potential: fear. It's time to tell yourself the truth about your fears. It's more than just worrying. Go deeper for positive change. Fear causes worry. Are you so afraid that you won't even try?

It may sound strange to say that fear and worry are comfortable to a lot of us. That is because uncertainty can be distressing. When every day feels the same, there are fewer risks for things to go wrong. Some people feel threatened by the unknown. But…

When everything stays the same, you remain the same with no growth. If you don't take chances, try something new, or do anything outside of your comfort zone, you can't go next-level. So if you are not evolving but feeling "okay," it is because you have mistaken lack of growth for stability. Dynamic women do not shrink themselves to make other people feel better.

Get comfortable being uncomfortable as you prepare to make big moves. The next level is waiting for you. You don't have to accept a mediocre anything if you don't want to. Instead of being nervous, you can feel excited and hopeful with possibilities. Then you can gain so much more.

Affirmation

> **I have no fear or hesitation in accepting my unique path to success.**

Holistic Prescription

Call to Action

Develop your support system for the psychological safety you need to focus on your goals.

Mother Nature

Use these herbs and flowers: rose for increasing love vibrations, including self-love; cedarwood for positive new beginnings; clove for physical stimulation and positive energy attraction.

Gemstones

Activate these gemstones: tiger's eye for increasing confidence while releasing fear and anxiety; citrine for enhanced manifestation, personal will, and prosperity; and onyx for absorbing and transforming negative energy, plus increasing emotional and physical strength.

Feng Shui

For optimal feng shui balance and harmony: Add earth colors yellow and orange for stability; add metal colors white and gray and metal furnishings for integrity, joy, beauty, and clarity; add water elements like ocean artwork and circular shapes for prosperity and wisdom; add fire elements like candles and the color red for passion, dynamic energy, and brilliance.

61

DEFEAT DOUBT

Doubt is like a little pest that you thought you exterminated, but then, wait…there it is again. You and doubt may be old friends, but you don't have to see it again if you don't want to. You can defeat doubt when you listen to your own authentic voice, not to the naysayers and those trying to benefit from your insecurities.

Maybe you are nervous because you are starting something new. Starting something new is creating something from nothing. It's a bold move. Anything can happen. That is what makes it exciting too. Doing something profoundly different is like taking a machete and cutting your way through a dense jungle. There are obstacles and challenges but also divine gifts and rewarding surprises.

No one can tell you how to be you. Your wants, your feelings, your experiences, and your mind are all unique. You are doing this because *only you* can. If it were good and easy, everybody would do it. Slay doubt like a dragon slayer. Tell it goodbye by doing this:

- Replace questions about *if you can* do something with affirmations about *how you can*.
- Surround yourself with people who cheer you on.
- Focus on what you will do after your achievement; not *if*, but *when*.
- Work with people who believe in you and your vision.
- Love people who believe in you and your vision.
- Be clear about what you want.
- Don't worry about or get caught up in the *how*.

Affirmation

> **I release all doubt and negativity from my life.**

Holistic Prescription

 Call to Action

Truly release *all* doubt with the affirmation. If you currently surround yourself with any doubters, ditch them all ASAP. Replace them with cheerleaders.

 Mother Nature

Use these herbs: allspice for self-awareness, emotional healing, and luck; sage for spiritual purification and new positive beginnings; and thyme for spiritual awareness, plus healing with love and courage.

 Gemstones

Activate these gemstones: tiger's eye for increasing confidence while releasing fear and anxiety; aventurine for nurturing yourself, bringing joy and a positive attitude; and blue agate for patience, peace, hope, and positive thinking.

 Feng Shui

For optimal feng shui balance and harmony: Add floor pillows for meditation and grounding; add the earth color orange for stability; add purple and gold colors to manifest prosperity; add wooden furnishings for growth, healing, and inspiration; add fire elements with white candles to promote dynamic energy, peace, and confidence.

62

DAYDREAM

Dreams are a window into another dimension on the soul level. A little-known fact: You can dream while you are sleeping *and* while you are awake. Daydreaming helps you explore your ideas without fear. If you are brave enough, there are no limits.

Your dreams are yours and yours alone. In your dream, there is no one to defeat you before you begin by telling you what you can and can't do.

Did someone used to kill your dreams? As an adult, you decide what your dreams are and how "realistic" they will be to achieve. But…did you know that you can kill your own dreams?

Maybe you hold in your mind an idea about your limitations and choose not to dream beyond those perceived limits. If so, that's sad. Because you own your dreams. If they die, it is because you choose not to nurture and develop them. Not because you are not capable. Maybe you have been afraid to try. With faith in yourself, you won't kill your dreams. Instead, you will dream wild, fantastic dreams. And with focus, hard work, and commitment, you can make them come true.

Daydreaming is creative visualization. It's purposeful imagination. According to Shakti Gawain, author of *Creative Visualization*, imagination is "the basic creative energy of the universe." Daydreaming will help you uncover new tools you never knew you had in order to achieve more.

In your dreamy vision, try to be as detailed as possible to get exactly what you want. Your positive intentions can create your positive reality but only when combined with your willful imagination. With daydreaming, you are empowered to create the story of your life.

Daydream for hours, minutes, or even seconds. You can do it whenever you want to fill a time gap with something special and good. Waiting for a friend in your car? Having trouble falling asleep? Distracted during meditation? Taking a break outside? Daydream away! You will never be bored again.

Affirmation

I dream to manifest my most beautiful, fulfilled, and exceptional life.

Holistic Prescription

 Call to Action
Practice. Wishing for more is not the same as manifesting. And mind wandering is just that, not so productive. Daydreaming is detailed focused visualization. Like most things, practice often to do it well. Maybe when you are ready, you will share your vision with someone special to gain support.

 Mother Nature
Use these herbs and flowers: allspice for self-awareness, emotional healing, and luck; jasmine for self-worth, beauty, and spiritual awareness; and rose for increasing love vibrations, including self-love.

 Gemstones
Activate these gemstones: amethyst for fortification and increased spiritual awareness; quartz crystal for purification and inspiring creativity; and aquamarine to clear the mind and connect to higher health and well-being.

 Feng Shui
For optimal feng shui balance and harmony: Add water elements like the color blue to increase connection and to go deeper; add metal furniture and accents to increase the beauty in your visioning process; add wood furnishings for growth.

63

WRITE FOR BALANCE

Are you practicing regular self-reflection? By tuning in and expressing ourselves, we achieve and maintain a healthy emotional state. Many of us call this "balance."

Expressing your emotions is the ultimate form of self-expression. There is no judgment here, only a listening ear. You can sort through your emotions and reap therapeutic benefits by writing in a journal. You will find creative and accessible ways to heal and find peace, primarily by writing.

I suggest that you buy a beautiful new journal and record your thoughts on at least three different dates. Then, read what you wrote after several days have passed. Do you feel better after you wrote in your journal? Do you still feel the same way as you did when you first wrote in it? What's changed since then? A lot can change in three days, three weeks, three months, or three years. Sometimes, we change our minds and feelings in three minutes!

You may also find it helpful to look at your journal to find patterns in your behavior and your relationships. Are you making better choices now? Why or why not?

Note your state of mind before you journal, and then after. What advice would you give to your past self? Apply that advice to the person you are now.

Journaling helps you realize where you have been and where you need to go and provides groundwork for charting your progress (or recognizing a lack thereof). In addition to expressing your thoughts at any given point in time, journals are also useful for making goals. Whether your goals are to achieve financial independence, lose weight, exercise more often, or get married, those blank pages are practically begging for specific strategies that will help make your dreams come true. Of course, this is useful not just for relaxation and letting go for balance, but for success and manifestation of your divine destiny.

Affirmation

> **In my safe space, I express all my feelings exactly as I feel them.**

Holistic Prescription

 Call to Action

When looking through old journals, have compassion for your past self and find ways to learn from her.

 Mother Nature

Use these herbs and flowers: amber for soothing and inspiring a carefree, optimistic disposition; gardenia for expansive healing and peaceful self-love; and thyme for spiritual awareness, plus healing with love and courage.

 Gemstones

Activate these gemstones: unakite for removing negativity and balancing emotions; kyanite for maximizing your full potential and uplifting self-expression; and malachite for transformation, clearing, balancing, soothing turbulent emotions, and calming rage.

 Feng Shui

For optimal feng shui balance and harmony: Clear all clutter in your home and work spaces; use soft lighting and textures to tone down the fire element; add earth elements and soothing colors like yellow and beige for grounding, self-care, and boundaries; add water colors blue and turquoise and journal near the sea, lake, or a water fountain to soothe yourself; use a metal bookmark and pretty flowers to increase beauty and joy.

Part Three

SPIRIT

Your spirit is your soul. Your body and mind are directionless without the soul; the soul tells your mind and body what to do. Spirit is the inner guide, a wise voice, your intuition. It carries you through and to your destiny. Your destiny is full of surprises and blessings that are specific and unique to you. You are already chosen.

In Parts 1 and 2, you learned how to use your body and mind to manifest effective chilling-out experiences. In Part 3, you will learn how to turn inward in order to be there for yourself. Just for you.

Cultural traditions, personal habits, and your concept of Spirit are inextricably linked. Know that Spirit is not religion and religion is not Spirit. No matter what your particular belief system may be, you will learn how to uplift your spirit and incorporate its helpful existence into your everyday life by choosing, tuning, creating, gaining, connecting, embracing, accessing, seeing, attracting, and elevating.

The key to chilling out and living a happy life is flexibility—accepting and adapting to change. How you let go of the need for control, move past difficulties, and work through bumps in the road is a sign of your character, who you really are, and what you are becoming. Your spirit is a powerful tool that can make this happen. Part 3 will show you how.

64

CHOOSE PEACE

Imagine that you are outside on a sunny, warm day. You are surrounded by leafy ferns, plentiful trees, and bright red rose bushes under a giant magnolia tree with huge, fragrant blooms all over it. Under your feet, you feel soft green grass. Here, you too are an amazing vision. Your skin is literally glowing.

You are free, like the queen of your castle in your own fantasyland. Here, in your most vivid imagination, you can energize your passions to bravely fight battles as the hero in your own story, dispensing justice to those who need it most. You can bring romantic notions to life, or you can just stare at the sky.

Imagine doing whatever brings you the most peaceful contentment, a feeling that you never even knew existed before. Treasure this moment. This is the foundation for your divine destiny as a peaceful warrior who knows how to be successful but also how to chill out and relax.

Most of us likely know this peaceful state naturally because it was our existence at least once before, even if that was before we were born. When we were in our mother's womb, we were at peace. In our protective cocoons, we were warm and fed, breathing and growing. No effort, no stress. Then, suddenly, we were thrust into the world. There was no turning back. Our lives started to include lots of effort and plenty of new experiences and stress. We believed that we couldn't be passively peaceful anymore. Instead, we bought into the busyness narrative. As independent and proactive people, many of us are searching to find this peaceful state again.

You have the power to choose peace. The power to choose peace is a state of mind *and* a state of body, *plus* a state of spirit. To truly unwind, our spirits must be contented. A contented state of being gives us both peace and stability.

According to Ralph Waldo Emerson, a highly regarded scholar on the connection between nature and spiritual self-discovery,

"Nothing can bring you peace but yourself." He wrote this sentence in 1841. However, the concept has been a universal practice in many ancient civilizations around the world. We must find this peace again if we want to be healthy and move forward with our lives.

Affirmation

Every day and in every way, I choose peace.

Holistic Prescription

 Call to Action

Embrace the power of knowing that peace is a daily choice and be patient. Developing inner peace is a process that can take some time.

 Mother Nature

Use these herbs: sage for spiritual purification and new positive beginnings; lavender for peaceful relaxation and restorative rest; and skullcap for releasing and relinquishing control.

 Gemstones

Activate these gemstones: blue agate for patience, peace, hope, and positive thinking; selenite for dispelling negative energy; and jade for wisdom, peace, heart energy, and harmony.

 Feng Shui

For optimal feng shui balance and harmony: Use earth colors yellow, brown, and tan to promote grounding, relaxation, and calm; add wood furnishings and the color green to promote healing; add water elements like circular furniture and a water fountain for relaxation and letting go.

65

TUNE IN TO PEACE

Do your daily check-in. What is your body feeling like today? Focus inward. Tune in. Find the peace.

During yoga, the resting state at the end is called Savasana, also known as corpse pose. During this time, some of us have wandering minds. Others start thinking about the tasks to be completed during the day. Others fall asleep. You should try to be somewhere in the dark space between fully conscious and not here at all. Aware. Non-thinking. Conscious. Still. Open. Breathing. Relaxed. Peaceful.

You are meant to be in this space, and in this state, you reap the greatest benefits. You can create, do, and be your best. If you are not there, something else is going on. That is, if you are not feeling at peace, there is likely something preventing you from being able to achieve it. An important aspect of finding your peace is identifying what is preventing you from being at peace. Sometimes it's your own self.

The best part: You don't have to try so hard. In fact, it's better (and easier) if you don't. This is your naturally peaceful place, the mental state where your key effortlessly opens the lock. Know that your peaceful place exists. It can be tempting to give up when you don't find it right away. But don't. Keep going. Don't give up until you find your chill.

Like the many stations on a radio or the many roads that lead to a certain place, there are many options available to you and many paths that can get you there. Some are more scenic, glamorous, and joyful than others. Eventually, you will be able to fine-tune your inner energy and pinpoint your exact preferred location to find your peace.

Experiment with new ways of being and doing, find what you are instinctively drawn to, and discover what brings you to the most relaxed state. Mark that station. Note the location. Put it on repeat.

Affirmation

> *Tuning inward, I find my peaceful place where I am calm, collected, knowledgeable, and balanced.*

Holistic Prescription

 Call to Action

Add peace to your daily schedule—write it in! Remember to go to your peaceful place when you start to feel any indicators of stress.

 Mother Nature

Use these herbs: thyme for spiritual awareness, plus healing with love and courage; passionflower to reduce restlessness, anxiety, and insomnia; and chamomile for calming relaxation.

 Gemstones

Activate these gemstones: fluorite for peace and increasing mental clarity; howlite for remaining true to yourself and to soothe emotions; and larimar for stillness, calm, and chilling vibes.

 Feng Shui

For optimal feng shui balance and harmony: Use earth colors like yellow, beige, and gold, plus wood furnishings to promote healing; add water elements like circular furniture and a water fountain for peace and calm; add the color black and visualize a soundproof black box to promote clarity, wisdom, and peace as you are tuning in.

66

STAY GROUNDED

Some days feel better than others. When things seem to be falling apart around you, you can stay together and still be yourself. Being grounded means being firmly rooted in who you are, in what you are becoming, and in your present reality, like a tree. When you are grounded, you are free from negativity and intense emotional disruptions, and you respond to change more easily without baggage or fear.

Think about your favorite ways to stay emotionally stable and balanced. What are your favorite things to do? Your process is your ritual. It's a great feeling to have such a healthy habit.

Just as you are encouraged to have a ritual to balance your emotions (see entry 58: Balance Emotions), you are encouraged to use rituals to stay grounded. A "ritual" may sound scary, but it's simply tapping in to our own power to serve our highest good. Ancient and effective, a ritual is a practice of self-care.

Like brushing your teeth or washing your hands, self-care rituals become your daily habits when you perform them without thinking about them. Your ritual may be meditation in the morning before coffee. An afternoon affirmation. A prayer at night before you go to sleep.

We all have moments when we are confused and disappointed, even unhinged and upset. A ritual is just the go-to activity when you feel like maybe you are losing your way. When you stay in ritual, you are grounded to the earth in your reality. Here, you can make a difference and evolve. You can be who you are and be an asset for others.

Staying grounded may mean doing nothing. Being still. Rooted firmly. Unwavering in spirit. Strong in ritual. In other situations, maybe you have to do a little more.

Staying grounded means tending to yourself, listening and responding to your body barometers, seeking and maintaining inner peace, obeying your soul voice, and so much more. It's so effective that you won't need a whole lot more.

What rituals have you performed this week? Your mental health depends on it.

Affirmation

I stay in ritual to stay grounded.

Holistic Prescription

 Call to Action

Use windows, artwork, and nature walks to coexist and walk with, and fully embrace, Mother Nature. Surround yourself with nature's wonder.

 Mother Nature

Use these herbs: sage for spiritual purification and new positive beginnings; juniper berries for releasing negativity; and cinnamon for grounding and balancing energy.

 Gemstones

Activate these gemstones: turquoise for health and inner calm; unakite for removing negativity and balancing emotions; and moss agate for increased immune functioning, happiness, and overall balance.

Feng Shui

For optimal feng shui balance and harmony: Clear clutter; add earth elements for grounding, self-care, and boundaries; add wood elements with green and teal colors, large wooden furnishings, and plants and flowers for growth and healing.

67

CREATE A PROTECTIVE SHIELD

Self-love and self-care are the keys to success. And the key to your protection. We protect ourselves by prioritizing first self-love and then self-care. By loving ourselves, we place our own care above the care of others (a controversial statement for some, but you will see why it is true).

Whether or not we realize it, we often search for the familiarity and comfort that we experienced during our earliest stages of life. Some of us create our own cocoons specifically for this purpose. This is especially true during our most difficult times. Maybe your cocoon is your bedroom....Usually there comes a time when you are supposed to emerge from your cocoon upgraded and improved, ready for the world. However, when it is time to come out of your cocoon, you may also feel more vulnerable and exposed. Recognizing your fears and gaining courage to overcome them always comes back inward toward the self. Maybe you need a little something more to feel more ready. You can change that feeling of vulnerability and weakness by learning to create and use a protective shield.

You can create your shield as a bubble or barrier, the thing that makes negativity bounce right off, the protective shield that makes you pretty invincible, undeterred, unfazed. Yours does not look like hers, and hers does not look like his. What does your shield look like?

Maybe yours is a literal visualization of a shield. Maybe it's a symbol of your power and protection, like an outfit, a piece of jewelry, a feather… a force field of radiating protective energy. It can be anything you choose. It's not about the object itself, but it is your soulful intention, your projection and manifestation, that makes it valuable and effective.

As women, we are often taught to rely on men to protect us. There are other protections available. With self-awareness, we understand the energy and the power of what we have and who we are. Just as we lock our doors to protect our loved ones and valuables or use an umbrella when it rains, we can protect our souls.

Affirmation

Holistic Prescription

 Call to Action

Visualize and practice erecting your force field when navigating unknown situations and negative people.

 Mother Nature

Use these herbs: bay leaves for spiritual enhancement and protection; peppermint for enhanced healing, luck, love, and protection; and thyme for spiritual awareness, plus healing with love and courage.

 Gemstones

Activate these gemstones: moonstone for self-protection and good fortune; citrine for enhanced manifestation, personal will, and prosperity; and onyx for absorbing and transforming negative energy, plus increasing emotional and physical strength.

 Feng Shui

For optimal feng shui balance and harmony: Add earth elements like clay pots and stones for grounding; add metal elements like metal furniture and mirrors, plus white and gray colors for increased clarity and precision; add water elements and the color blue for connection, wisdom, and increased intuition.

68

MAINTAIN INNER PEACE

Peace is gold. Does looking for your inner peace feel like looking for a needle in a haystack? It may be time to get growing. Let's take a look at that potential for growth.

A peaceful state can be hard-earned. For most of us, it doesn't just happen. By incorporating peaceful habits into your daily life, each day, one by one, you are building your peaceful lifestyle. It's a choice you make. Every. Day.

When you have achieved inner peace, you have everything you need to fulfill your dreams and the capacity to start anew. Every second is literally a new beginning. Know that the Universe will always take care of you. This knowledge can bring you comfort and peace too.

When you walk in the sun, lie down in the grass, and dance in your living room, you feel alive. Free. Unencumbered. When you are at ease, you are operating at your most authentic level; from this place, no matter how transient or fleeting the calm feeling may seem at the time, you are able to find moments of peace. You can hold onto that feeling and repeat it as often as possible. Sometimes we have to remind ourselves to slow down until it becomes a life-changing habit. Our very lives depend on us being able to find our peace.

We all breathe. In, out, in, out. Do this: Breathe in joy, breathe out tension. Breathe in opportunities, release anxiety. Breathe in dreams, release disappointment.

Inner peace is the key to being successful, happy, healthy, well rested, and emotionally balanced. Once you find it, keep doing the work to maintain it and you will reap the many rewards.

Affirmation

I have peace in my heart, peace in my life, and trust that I have everything I need right now in this moment.

Holistic Prescription

 Call to Action

Be prepared to do the work to achieve inner peace and to maintain it by embracing a regular practice that helps you achieve peace, such as meditation, yoga, breath work, therapy, regular meetings with your support team members, art, dance…whatever works. It's worth it!

 Mother Nature

Use these herbs and flowers: sage for spiritual purification and new positive beginnings; juniper berries for releasing negativity; and gardenia for expansive healing and peaceful self-love.

 Gemstones

Activate these gemstones: blue agate for patience, peace, hope, and positive thinking; selenite for dispelling negative energy; and labradorite for intuition and to protect your aura.

 Feng Shui

For optimal feng shui balance and harmony: Use earth colors yellow, brown, and tan to promote relaxation and calm; add wood furnishings to promote healing; add water elements, such as circular shapes and regular baths, for relaxation and letting go.

69

GAIN COURAGE

You have support, guidance, and love, so, really, what are you waiting for? Put yourself where you want to be. It's not wishful thinking but action that supports your destiny, and the Universe is designed to assist. When things are going great, sometimes we get scared. It's understandable. Maybe you are still learning to reprogram old beliefs and thought patterns that we have been taught; learning to unlearn. Instead of worrying, which shrinks your hopes and dreams, be brave. Trust…

Courage is not the absence of fear. It's moving forward despite it. As women, we have always had courage. Courage to love, heal, give, receive, carry on, succeed, march, fight, and persevere. Because being courageous is not just about doing certain things. It's about making choices, affirming your authenticity, and maintaining your cool.

If you are feeling in need of encouragement or are too afraid to achieve your dreams right now, ask yourself, "What am I afraid of?" The answer may surprise you. Work on conquering that fear and in doing so, you will develop the courage to be exactly what you need.

Just when you think you might have to shrink your business, close a door, or cease operations, do the opposite. Aim higher. Which means…go for it! The stars, the moon are all waiting. Why play safe and small when you have what it takes to be grand? Develop the confidence to know your worth. The people who love you will always love you and support your goals.

Reach higher and higher until you don't recognize where you are anymore. Then, don't panic. Be steady. You've been ready for this for a long time. Conquer the fear to understand that this is your path. You are what you have been waiting for.

Affirmation

Holistic Prescription

 Call to Action

Process your fears. Don't be afraid of fear; work through the things that you are afraid of.

 Mother Nature

Use these herbs and flowers: allspice for self-awareness, emotional healing, and luck; clove for physical stimulation and positive energy attraction; and honeysuckle for beauty, personal power, and self-love.

 Gemstones

Activate these gemstones: tiger's eye for increasing confidence while releasing fear and anxiety; garnet for chi stimulation and to remove emotional blockages in the body; and apatite for willpower and strength through love.

 Feng Shui

For optimal feng shui balance and harmony: Use green, blue, and teal colors for the energy of new beginnings to start new projects and personal growth; use the color purple to manifest prosperity, self-worth, and financial abundance; add wood and fire elements for growth, healing, and inspiration—for example, a small, wooden meditation table with white candles.

70

INTRODUCE SOUL LOGIC

There's mind logic, body logic, and soul logic. You need them all. Soul logic is the inner voice that tells the truth and can't be tricked; the reasons why, even when you can't explain; the thing that keeps you going despite the obstacles; and what makes others wonder, "How did she do that?"

The great thing about soul logic is that you don't need to know the how or the why. That knowledge is so unnecessary, because you can just do it. Knowing can be freeing and so liberating! But only if you allow it to do what it is supposed to do.

Our minds are amazing, but they are not all there is. And we are constantly being bombarded by information. The mind can be manipulated by external stimuli and will be utterly directionless without the soul. Soul logic is the key; it explains the mind-body connection.

Do you hear your soul talking to you, making all that good sense? The soul intuitively knows what your mind is trying to tell you. If you focus on what is right in front of you, less about your environment and your appearance, you can see and feel it.

What makes you feel most useful, loved, and respected? This is a large part of your soul logic. When you are doing what you love and living your purpose with those around you, your life just flows and makes sense. This type of reasoning may yield different advice than listening to others whom you love, trust, and respect. Still, know that the soul knows best.

Affirmation

I trust the principles that guide my soul to stay in destiny on purpose.

Holistic Prescription

 ### Call to Action
When you are examining the pros and cons of a situation, remember to include soul logic in the equation.

 ### Mother Nature
Use these herbs and flowers: thyme for spiritual awareness, plus healing with love and courage; jasmine for self-worth, beauty, and spiritual awareness; and peppermint for enhanced healing, luck, love, and protection.

 ### Gemstones
Activate these gemstones: jade for wisdom, peace, heart energy, and harmony; amethyst for fortification and increased spiritual awareness; and lapis for wisdom and serene awareness.

 ### Feng Shui
For optimal feng shui balance and harmony: Clear clutter to hear your soul's voice more clearly; add water elements, such as circular shapes, water fountains, paintings of the sea, and dark blue and black colors to increase connection to your soul and spiritual awareness; visit the sea.

71

LISTEN TO YOUR SOUL

It's one thing to have soul logic. It's another thing to actually listen to it, to put it to use in order to enhance your daily life. Maybe you could use a brief reminder of what it means to listen to your soul. Can you hear it?

Your soul loves to rest, relax, be present, and let go. When someone asks you what you're doing, you can proudly say, "Nothing much," "Chillin," "Relaxing," or "Chillaxing." But really, you are doing so much more. You are listening to your soul.

When you act consistently with what your soul wants to do, you are living an authentic life full of promise. It doesn't matter what you did in the past or who you used to be. Your spiritual elevation is right here, right now. With newfound awareness, you can consistently tap in to Spirit. It helps you on a micro level (day-to-day) and a macro level (uplifting your whole life).

Where is your inner voice? Listen to that voice inside that speaks to you all the time. It is your intuition; your responsibility is to listen and act. Your soul likes and needs to be listened to. Listening to your soul helps you detect the clues that it's time to chill out and enjoy the present. Your safe spaces honor and protect your soul while you evolve, like a cocoon. What is your cocoon?

How many of us are thriving and succeeding on the outside, only to be barely surviving or teetering on the edge of a medical catastrophe on the inside? Why wait for your body to fail before acting in your own best interest? Now, you can listen to your soul.

Listen to your soul by following soul logic. Soul logic explains the mind-body connection. Do you understand what your soul is trying to tell you? Your soul looks out for you in the most ultimate ways. It wants you to be happy. It wants you to be healthy. It wants the best for you. It wants you to learn but not suffer too much in the process. It wants you to receive but also give. It wants you to show up for yourself and for others. It wants you to lead, teach, and serve. It wants you to come full circle in your lifetime with no regrets.

Affirmation

> **Chilling out, I listen to my soul voice to exist in peaceful harmony with myself and my surroundings.**

Holistic Prescription

 Call to Action

Identify special spaces where you can listen carefully to what your soul has to say.

 Mother Nature

Use these herbs and flowers: thyme for spiritual awareness, plus healing with love and courage; honeysuckle for beauty, personal power, and self-love; and bay leaves for spiritual enhancement and protection.

 Gemstones

Activate these gemstones: amethyst for fortification and increased spiritual awareness; kyanite for maximizing your full potential and uplifting self-expression; and lepidolite for attracting love, hope, and light, plus change acceptance.

 Feng Shui

For optimal feng shui balance and harmony: Clear clutter; review your space in terms of the five elements (water, wood, earth, metal, fire); remove everything except the items that absolutely speak to your soul and bring joy.

72

CONNECT TO SPIRIT

Do you look around and wonder "How did I get here?" You are not the only one. Where life takes us is a mystery, an adventure that we were born to partake in. Our spirits are leading the way. The line is not always straight, but Spirit says to be faithful and deliberate. When you are feeling like maybe you lost your way, you can connect and reconnect to Spirit. For some, prayer and meditation can help. Others find Spirit in nature or by retreating with like-minded women.

Many of us focus on communication when what we really want in our lives is connection. There's such a big difference between communicating—look at social media—and connecting. Connecting is how we bond in our most valuable relationships. Before we connect to other people, we must first establish that deep connection with ourselves. By connecting to Spirit.

Don't despair if you realize that you've been trying to get the wrong thing! Let's prioritize it and you will only notice improvements in the quality of your entire life. With Spirit, you are never alone. How do you make the connection? Nature helps you connect. Whenever possible, plan your personal and professional life around your need to be regularly immersed in a natural environment. Try to:

- Acknowledge your intuition as Spirit talking to you.
- Walk in nature to clear your heart and open your mind to Spirit.
- Meditate to hear what Spirit has to tell you.
- See your path as one that is charted by Spirit.
- Ask specifically for what you need.
- Understand that your spirit knows and understands you better than anyone.
- Trust in what Spirit is telling you, especially in your dreams.

Affirmation

I listen and trust my spirit to guide me toward the life that is wonderful and perfect for me.

Holistic Prescription

 Call to Action

Focusing on what you are grateful for helps you connect to Spirit. You can do this in meditation.

 Mother Nature

Use these herbs and flowers: bay leaves for spiritual enhancement and protection; thyme for spiritual awareness, plus healing with love and courage; and rose for increasing love vibrations, including self-love.

 Gemstones

Activate these gemstones: sodalite for getting in tune with your intuition and higher consciousness; jade for wisdom, peace, heart energy, and harmony; and aquamarine to clear the mind and connect to higher health and well-being.

 Feng Shui

For optimal feng shui balance and harmony: Clear all clutter; use furnishings with tables and chairs that force people to face each other—for example, a circular table—because circles are a water element that increases therapeutic connection, healing, and growth; meditate on a floor cushion for grounding using earth colors yellow, brown, and tan; add wood elements with plants for spiritual nourishment.

73

INCREASE SELF-AWARENESS

Know thyself. No truer words have been spoken than those of this ancient proverb. We tell ourselves to be productive with our work. We tell ourselves to be good mothers, aunts, sisters, and daughters. We tell ourselves to be good partners for our significant others. We tell ourselves to be tidy, get organized, be pretty and sexy, be kind and diplomatic, maintain availability and responsiveness to others, all while being encouraged to stay in great shape and manifest our own wildest dreams.

Well…how has this been working for you? Many of us are frustrated and really, really *tired*. Of course. Who wouldn't be? Like many women, maybe you feel overwhelmed, overworked, misled, taken advantage of, and—perhaps most importantly—your soul is undernourished because… Maybe you don't truly know yourself. You thought you did. You think you do, but nope.

Did you have that experience? How did you feel about it? Why do you do what you do? When you open the book to your life, what does it say? What does it all mean? Well, to quote the unlikeliest source, the TV series *The Walking Dead*, "Self-awareness is a beautiful thing." Some say self-awareness is the most attractive and awe-inspiring trait that a person can have.

Start with who you are, where you're from, what motivates you, what you love, whom you love, what you fight for, what is sacred for you, what you value, and how you live your life. Then, go deeper. Examine your shadow side, the parts that other people don't see and the less obvious aspects of yourself that you push down and try to hide. You don't have to be afraid, and there are no judgments about good or bad. Self-knowledge is not perfection. Loving yourself completely means accepting yourself unconditionally. All of you.

To get more familiar with all aspects of yourself, continue learning to be still. Treat yourself like you treat a new friend or lover.

Explore, listen, and note what's new. Meditating daily, starting with five minutes, gradually adding one minute each week can help too.

Affirmation

> **I learn something new, exciting, and wonderful about myself each day.**

Holistic Prescription

 ### Call to Action
Use your journal as the best tool to increase knowledge of yourself.

 ### Mother Nature
Use these herbs: allspice for self-awareness, emotional healing, and luck; clove for physical stimulation and positive energy attraction; and rosemary for purified physical healing love.

 ### Gemstones
Activate these gemstones: fluorite for peace and increasing mental clarity; citrine for enhanced manifestation, personal will, and prosperity; and spinel for hope, gratitude, and appreciation to realign your life.

 ### Feng Shui
For optimal feng shui balance and harmony: Clear clutter; add earth elements like ceramics and stones to increase knowledge and wisdom; include books and pictures of people you admire; use the fire color red to stimulate interest and energy; use the color pink for compassion.

74

LEARN WHAT YOUR SPIRIT NEEDS

In addition to connecting to Spirit in nature, you can process your own personal stories yourself to maintain a peaceful state of mind. Writing in your journal can help you learn exactly what your spirit needs and when. As a bonus, the journal is a historical record of what happened—when, how, where, and what you did, said, felt, and experienced. When you journal, you are processing your life in that particular moment and capturing it as a snapshot in time. This historical record is helpful as you embark on your self-awareness and self-development journey.

I know…your feelings can run deep. Your emotional responses can cause imbalance. Mine too. Fortunately, they become more temporary and shorter in duration when you process your feelings in a healthy way. Journaling can help you work through it. In this way, it prevents you from getting stuck in that space, a black hole of anger, rage, and frustration. Journals help you to successfully navigate through your experiences and resurface for air instead of allowing them to define you and influence you in a negative way.

Later, when you look back at the journal, you can see how temporary your chaotic state of mind really was. And how you needed to *feel* it to *release* it. Phew! You got through it, after all. Now, you are more familiar with what your spirit wants and needs. It wants you to use this experience to grow.

Spirit gravitates toward what is joyful and healthy. Learning what your soul needs is more important than learning to read and write, which we do in first grade. Try to make your spiritual needs just as important. I know that most of us have to make up for the fact that we were not taught how to do it when we were younger. We must take the initiative to learn as quickly as we can right now.

When you make your spiritual needs a priority, you will find the way. Eventually, it will become an automatic consideration with everything you do. Remember: It's holistic, and everything is connected.

Our spirits are connected, too, in our oneness. Like family, the members of your spiritual community are out there, waiting to be found.

Affirmation

As I learn and grow, moving closer to Spirit, I am joyful and healthy.

Holistic Prescription

 ### Call to Action

Treat the people around you as members of a connected spiritual family who help each other learn and grow.

 ### Mother Nature

Use these herbs and flowers: sage for spiritual purification and new positive beginnings; jasmine for self-worth, beauty, and spiritual awareness; and rosemary for purified physical healing love.

 ### Gemstones

Activate these gemstones: amethyst for fortification and increased spiritual awareness; chrysoprase to help you recognize the grace and beauty in yourself; and quartz crystal for purification and inspiring creativity.

 ### Feng Shui

For optimal feng shui balance and harmony: Use earth and wood elements like wood furniture and plants for grounding and healing; burn incense that includes sage, jasmine, and rosemary to enhance connection; maintain balance of all five elements: water, wood, earth, metal, and fire with furnishings, plants, artwork, and colors.

75

BECOME A FORCE OF NATURE

Is there a way to become a force of nature? Yes, there is. First, know that you already are. Second, let yourself be who you are. Third, enhance what's there.

There's a time to chill and a time to be a force of nature. Mother Nature comforts and soothes with stillness. She also gives us hurricanes and tornados. Our duality makes us interesting, unique, and whole.

We are nature. All of us. Your soul taps into your humanity and what it really means to be a force of nature, connected to the whole, linked to the rest of the human race and the planet. Tap in to your superpower to become a force of nature. It's time to embrace your wild side. You can unleash your natural power now. It's okay to let it all out. At the same time, you gotta learn to chill.

Look at forests. Walking among large, tall trees will give you proper perspective: in comparison to their size and grandeur, you are like a tiny speck of dust in a wide-open space. The same concept of scale also applies to mountains: when you see the majesty of mountains, it's amazingly beautiful. Look at the vast, open sea. Understand the miracle of creation, the depths of which we know virtually nothing about.

Humbling, isn't it? You quicky realize that the world is not always just about you. But you are part of this world too. With renewed perspective, you can focus on removing any self-imposed pressure to do or be something else other than who and what you are.

We can learn so much from just one tree. Mighty trees are long-lived, resilient, adaptable, and firmly rooted yet bending and yielding to survive. This is how trees can survive different seasons, storms, and natural disasters. Aspire to be like a tree. Just like you, it is a force of nature. It is just one of many. We are too.

When you walk, you do not walk alone. We are part of Mother Nature's majesty. *You* are majestic, mighty, and amazing too. Chances are, you wasted precious time blending into the background. Not anymore.

Affirmation

Intense, intentional, limitless, and powerful, I am a feminine force of nature.

Holistic Prescription

 Call to Action

Honored and humbled by the majesty of nature, find the people who are honored and humbled to be around you in the same way.

 Mother Nature

Use these herbs and flowers: thyme for spiritual awareness, plus healing with love and courage; honeysuckle for beauty, personal power, and self-love; and clove for physical stimulation and positive energy attraction.

 Gemstones

Activate these gemstones: citrine for enhanced manifestation, personal will, and prosperity; jade for wisdom, peace, heart energy, and harmony; and tiger's eye for increasing confidence while releasing fear and anxiety.

 Feng Shui

For optimal feng shui balance and harmony: Add the fire color red for confidence, strength, and courage; add water colors green, blue, and teal for the energy of new beginnings to start new projects and personal growth and to manifest the power of the ocean; add wood accents and the fire element sunshine for growth, healing, and inspiration.

76

NURTURE YOUR SOUL

Your soul is a sun. Sometimes we get down on ourselves for not doing more or being more. This is an act of self-hatred and sabotage. What you do with your time, your talent, and your physical self is up to you. How you nurture your soul is your business. Just like you don't need a gym to be fit, you don't need a job to serve. All you need is yourself, really. Ask yourself these questions:

- How do I show up in service?
- How do I nurture my soul?
- Am I okay with me?

Everything around you emanates from within you, shining on the world like a bright light. The sun doesn't have an obligation to everything and everybody it touches. Neither do you. If anything, it's the opposite—everybody and everything that is touched by the sun knows that this energy is special. When you derive special benefit from something or someone, we have an obligation to honor and protect this precious gift.

Are the people around you honoring and protecting you? Teach them how. Show them the way by honoring yourself. Do you know the best way to honor yourself? We honor ourselves by nurturing our souls with (1) self-knowledge, (2) self-love, and (3) boundaries.

Let's make it a priority. When you get to know, love, and appreciate every part of yourself, you will find out who she really is.

Affirmation

> **Knowing myself and treating myself well, I nurture my soul and honor my life path.**

Holistic Prescription

 Call to Action

Surround yourself only with people who honor, protect, and nurture you.

 Mother Nature

Use these herbs and flowers: bay leaves for spiritual enhancement and protection; jasmine for self-worth, beauty, and spiritual awareness; and gardenia for expansive healing and peaceful self-love.

 Gemstones

Activate these gemstones: moss agate for increased immune functioning, happiness, and overall balance; aventurine for nurturing yourself, bringing joy and a positive attitude; and pyrite for transformative healing.

 Feng Shui

For optimal feng shui balance and harmony: Clear all clutter; use the color gold to manifest the power of the sun for positive energy and grounding; use water elements like circular designs to encourage natural flow, deep wisdom, and connection; add fire elements with sunshine.

77

CREATE SACRED SPACES

By definition, safe spaces are sacred spaces. And sacred spaces are safe spaces. We can chill out only when we know for sure that we are safe. A safe place is a place to begin. Sacred spaces are about peace of mind. They are not related specifically to a physical location—which is how you are able to find them over and over again, anywhere you are and whenever you want to.

Our home is the ultimate sacred space for most of us. The benefits of *wellness real estate* in our daily lives is often overlooked. The importance of how women create a home for themselves is also underestimated. Wellness is a state of mind, body, spirit, culture, and tradition. Being in a depressed and anxious environment makes you feel depressed and anxious. That's how energy works. Today, there are opportunities to incorporate wellness real estate principles to create sacred spaces.

It makes perfect sense that many of us also find sacred spaces in nature. They are abundant! A little spot under the tree by the shoreline. A short cliff on the side of the mountain. The bench in the backyard under the cherry tree. There is a spot with your name on it, waiting for you to claim it. Being around nature is not just eco-friendly (a big plus!); it is required to be healthier. It's so amazing that safe spaces are also healthy. Wellness real estate can be achieved at all income levels and home settings. How we live and interact with Mother Nature is the foundation of holistic health and emotional well-being.

Where is your sacred space? It is the place from which you emerge to navigate the demands of the material world. Here, you can renew, restore, regenerate, and replenish yourself.

Affirmation

I achieve inner peace, elevation, and joy in my personal sacred space.

Holistic Prescription

 Call to Action

Define what is required for your safe space.

 Mother Nature

Use these herbs: cinnamon for grounding and balancing energy; peppermint for enhanced healing, luck, love, and protection; and rosemary for purified physical healing love.

 Gemstones

Activate these gemstones: carnelian for strength, self-worth, and confidence; onyx for absorbing and transforming negative energy, plus increasing emotional and physical strength; and moonstone for self-protection and good fortune.

 Feng Shui

For optimal feng shui balance and harmony: Surround yourself with what you love; add metal accents for joy and beauty; add wood elements with the color green for growth and healing and white, pink, and gray for soothing, loving, yin energy; use candles to add fire.

78

BECOME PEACE

A contented disposition full of infinite possibility and unlimited potential is a special place. What is this special place called? You can call it whatever you want. Some people call this state of relaxation and stability "happiness" or "bliss," but it is peace.

How can you achieve this peaceful state? To get there, you have to chill out—the process of letting things be—with the understanding that you can handle whatever comes your way. Now that you've used the previous entries to help you find your sacred spots and learn to use Mother Nature to heal, you are empowered with love and light. Empowered to find your peace. Inner peace includes states of relaxation throughout the day and night, 24/7, 100 percent, mind, body, and spirit.

Change is awesome, and new beginnings are special. During and in-between, you can find peace. Expecting change, you are not thrown off balance when things do not go as planned. When something breaks. When energy shifts. When your world gets turned upside-down. The road curves and crossroads appear. Keep going. Not always knowing exactly what's ahead, get excited, not scared. Curious, not avoidant. Be triumphant, not defeated.

It doesn't matter what anyone else is doing or thinking. Your peace is there. It's your destiny to become it.

Affirmation

I become more peaceful every day, no matter what.

Holistic Prescription

 Call to Action

Start each day with a meditation or prayer for inner peace. Take notes and notice how you show up when you have it.

 Mother Nature

Use these herbs: sage for spiritual purification and new positive beginnings; rosemary for purified physical healing love; and lavender for peaceful relaxation and restorative rest.

 Gemstones

Activate these gemstones: amber for soothing and inspiring a carefree, optimistic disposition; blue agate for patience, peace, hope, and positive thinking; and lapis for wisdom and serene awareness.

 Feng Shui

For optimal feng shui balance and harmony: Clear all clutter; add earth colors tan and beige for grounding; use wood and fire elements, such as a wooden meditation table with a white candle, to promote healing and vitality; add water elements like circular furniture and a water fountain for relaxation and letting go, and visit the water regularly—for example, a lake, the ocean, a stream, or river.

79

FIND YOUR SPOT

Have you ever had a special place outdoors that was just for you? This is your Spot. You can meditate here, exercise, draw, journal, or do anything you want in this special sacred space.

Have you ever gotten lost alone in the woods? Excited and frightened, maybe you had no cell phone service and no visible way out. Are you giddy with excitement or really concerned about not knowing exactly where you are? This is what it's like to go looking for your Spot.

Spot-seeking, you are becoming a true wanderer in the woods, a real badass survivalist, a woman blazing her own trail and settling, finally, in her own Spot. The epitome of empowerment!

Maybe your special place is the beach. Here, you breathe in the salty air, the seawater sprays your skin, and your heartbeat slows down. Your skin glows from ocean spray and the warmth of the sun. Your body is quickly cooled by the gentle trade winds.

You feel so positive, healthy, and aware at your Spot. Every time you come here, you can feel your body literally settle down and decompress like a big sigh of relief. Here, it is easy to pause and chill out. Here, you are at home and at peace.

Your rhythm, your Spot. Have you found it yet? You will know that you found your Spot when:

- You feel safe and at peace.
- Daydreaming, visualizing, and manifesting come easily.
- The seating area seems specifically made for you and your body.
- It is easily accessible to you.

All you have to do is show up and wait for the magic to begin. Where is your Spot?

Affirmation

Holistic Prescription

 Call to Action

Choose a Spot full of positive energy, so intense that you can feel it right away.

 Mother Nature

Use these herbs: juniper berries for releasing negativity; clove for physical stimulation and positive energy attraction; and lemon balm for physical restoration.

 Gemstones

Activate these gemstones: moss agate for increased immune functioning, happiness, and overall balance; aventurine to bring joy, acceptance, and well-being; and ruby for healing and positive energy recovery.

 Feng Shui

For optimal feng shui balance and harmony: Clear all clutter; replicate the five elements by bringing the outdoors in, incorporating water, wood, earth, metal, and fire with plants, furnishings, colors, and accessories; focus on items that bring you the most peace and personal satisfaction.

80

OVERCOME LONELINESS

Divorces, breakups, affairs, ended friendships, and relationships that have simply outlived their usefulness are part of the change as we move in a new direction and discover what we really need and want from those around us, and from our lives in general. By understanding this process, we can accept the changes, adapt to them, and relax about them. So, chill out, knowing that this is part of what we are all going through right now.

If you only focus on the yearning of your heart and soul, you might spend endless hours suffering while searching for strategies and techniques that work for you. You don't have to. There is a difference between being alone and being lonely.

It is a positive and healthy choice to enjoy your own company. Solitude is a great path to self-knowledge and inner peace. Loneliness is a longing for companionship that can leave you feeling sad, wanting, and needing something outside of yourself. Loneliness seeks validation from external sources.

I know that it may be difficult to be alone sometimes. You overcome loneliness when you know intuitively that you are never really alone.

Try this: First, surround yourself with beauty and love. Those who support you and love you are the only ones that matter. Maybe you have good, like-minded connections in those who wholly embrace you. Even if it's just one person. Find them and do something special together when you are feeling a little down.

Second, don't forget to get or give yourself the hug that you need when you have challenges. Humans are not the only ones who provide positive energy. Our furry friends help us connect to our own divine nature and build resilience by decreasing loneliness. So much joy here!

Third, dream of the future you want to have, being clear about who you want to be with. Note the setting, colors, smells, and all the sensations that you see and feel. This is an important part of the creative visualization and manifestation process.

Affirmation

> *I enjoy the time I spend in solitude and selectively choose the company I keep.*

Holistic Prescription

 Call to Action

When you daydream about quality companionship, write down all the details (as many as possible!) in your journal. Use creative visualization regularly.

 Mother Nature

Use these herbs: juniper berries for releasing negativity; clove for physical stimulation and positive energy attraction; and yarrow for protecting and raising the frequency of love vibrations.

 Gemstones

Activate these gemstones: rose quartz for warm, caring, gentle self-love and emotional healing by releasing resentments; rhodonite for stimulating, clearing, and activating the heart; and malachite for purification and attracting love by opening the heart.

 Feng Shui

For optimal feng shui balance and harmony: Clear clutter; decorate with pairs of items, especially in your bedroom; maintain an ancestor altar with pictures of deceased loved ones; meditate about companionship to choose the right ones; at home, post pictures of those who love you.

81

EMBRACE NATURE

How did we get so far removed, so alienated from nature? When did we cease remembering to stop and smell the flowers? No matter how far away we are, we can always get back. We grow by observing the world, learning, adapting, and relaxing. This is exactly what we must do every day to grow and self-actualize. Because it is a natural process, Mother Nature is here to help us.

Did you know that simply touching and feeling plants can help you feel better? Yes, it really is that easy to enhance your mood, have a better day, and increase health. Just by embracing nature. Don't just stroll the grounds, although that is a great start. Embracing means to touch, to feel, to absorb the essence. When we embrace, we are open, willing, and accepting. We display enthusiastic affection and give thanks for what we receive. If we knew how helpful our natural environment was and interacted with Mother Nature more often, maybe we would think twice about destroying it. The implications are huge, not just for our everyday lives, but for our planet's existence.

With that in mind, try *forest bathing*. This Japanese tradition of using all your senses to experience nature releases bottled-up tension and takes you instantly to a place of peaceful calm and serenity. This is the inner peace that we are all seeking. And it's right in front of us. No bathing suit required!

You don't need to buy a thing or pay someone a professional fee to experience this bliss. Just go beyond. More than working. More than walking. More than hiking. More than going outside. See more than you have before. Feel better than ever. Finally…chill.

Your natural setting does not have to be a literal forest; you can go to a lake, a wooded area, a hiking trail, or any green space that is quiet (the more secluded, the better) to reap the benefits. Just don't forget to touch *and* smell the flowers.

Affirmation

Holistic Prescription

 Call to Action

Create indoor and outdoor garden areas to access Her gifts at all times.

 Mother Nature

Use these herbs and flowers: gardenia for expansive healing and peaceful self-love; peppermint for enhanced healing, luck, love, and protection; and rosemary for purified physical healing love.

 Gemstones

Activate these gemstones: amethyst for fortification and increased spiritual awareness; onyx for absorbing and transforming negative energy, plus increasing emotional and physical strength; and hematite for physical healing.

 Feng Shui

For optimal feng shui balance and harmony: Go outdoors every day and observe the five elements (water, wood, earth, metal, fire); bring these elements into your home in a balanced way with equal elements reflected in each living and working area; bring in as many living, moving elements as possible, such as plants and moving water, to represent the natural movements of life.

82

ACCESS JOY

Joy is wealth. When we talk about people being rich or poor, what do we really mean? With wisdom, we recognize wealth as a relative term, and it isn't all about money. Maybe if we focus on how wealthy we already are, we can be happy and access joy regularly.

Your spirit wants to roll around in joy, to feel good without worrying about anything. When we are feeling down, we often call it depression. Depression is a clinical diagnosis in which patients are often given prescription medication. Depression can often be accompanied by a lack of joy. But which one comes first: feeling depressed or the loss of joy?

Maybe it is our spirits that are depressed. Maybe your spirit is feeling a bit hidden or overwhelmed. Maybe it lost its way....Try something new by listening to what Spirit is telling you. Then, give it what it is asking for: more joy.

You see, joy is a *need*. Without it, we suffer. Just as there are medications for depression and tips for increasing monetary wealth, thank goodness there are healing prescriptions to increase joy.

Going beyond plants, trees, and flowers, animals intrigue us with their moods, presence, and playful energy. Interacting with dogs and cats can reduce stress, anxiety, and depression. Playing with our pets gives us more joyful energy. Watching wild animals like birds and marine life can also help us to appreciate life and relax. Their infectious positive energy helps us feel good!

Feeling joyful gives us hope for the future. Here are a few other ways to access joy:

- Maintaining inner peace and rest
- Prioritizing fun
- Enjoying quality food and shelter
- Planning and dreaming about a wonderful future

Affirmation

Holistic Prescription

 Call to Action

Service and joy are not mutually exclusive; feel good about helping others and cultivating a sharp mind.

 Mother Nature

Use these herbs: clove for physical stimulation and positive energy attraction; thyme for spiritual awareness, plus healing with love and courage; and yarrow for protecting and raising the frequency of love vibrations.

 Gemstones

Activate these gemstones: alexandrite for identifying and developing joy within yourself; aventurine for nurturing yourself, bringing joy and a positive attitude; and garnet for chi stimulation and to remove emotional blockages in the body.

 Feng Shui

For optimal feng shui balance and harmony: Use flowers to increase beauty and joy, especially rose, gardenia, jasmine, honeysuckle, and orchid; add metallic colors gold and silver (metal element); add joyful colors, such as bright yellow (earth) and red and fiery orange (fire).

83

RELEASE TENSION WITH THE SEA

Ocean tides are pulled back out to sea by the gravitational force of the moon. The tides of the ocean are synchronized with the changing rhythms of our lives: The same ocean can be predictable and unpredictable, fast and slow, large and small, exciting and calm, warm and cool, neat and messy at different times in different seasons. Maybe this sounds very much like your biography!

We can let the ocean waters heal us, absorb and take away our troubles, reduce stress and tension. We are not just doing this to feel better. Of course, what we are doing is much deeper than that: We are creating a healthy, stable foundation from which we can prepare ourselves to do anything we want and need to do.

When we see and hear water, we recognize an important part of ourselves. It's like our collective unconscious recognizes that life as we know it started as tiny organisms that materialized, grew, and developed in water. Water takes the shape of whatever contains it. It is also a carrier of everything. Spiritually, water is a carrier of our past and emotions. Fortunately for us, seawater cleanses and heals.

The impact of immersing yourself in a natural environment like the sea can be exponentially increased when you focus specifically on relaxation and letting go. When we want to let go of past hurt and traumatic experiences, we can baptize ourselves in these exceptional healing waters—and when we emerge, we are renewed, and even reborn. It is no wonder that spiritual baths and baptisms help us to start life over again; the sea allows us to press the reset button.

You can use water for renewal in an exercise that I call "The Sea Will Set You Free" (see the Call to Action in this entry). So, whenever you want to, you can use water to go back to the source of healing.

Affirmation

Like the waves of the sea washing over me, I heal my mind, body, and spirit in a most powerful way.

Holistic Prescription

 ### Call to Action

Go to the sea. (If you can't get to the actual ocean, think of your bathtub or shower as a mini ocean.) After meditating for a few moments, and expressing gratitude for all that you are grateful for, wade into the water. If you can, submerge your whole body underwater and speak the things you want to release into the water by saying, "I release [whatever you want to release]."

 ### Mother Nature

Use these herbs: skullcap for releasing and relinquishing control; sage for spiritual purification and new positive beginnings; and juniper berries for releasing negativity.

 ### Gemstones

Activate these gemstones: lapis for wisdom and serene awareness; rhodonite for emotional clearing from shock, trauma, and emotional wounds to achieve balance, self-love, and self-compassion; and turquoise for health and inner calm.

 ### Feng Shui

For optimal feng shui balance and harmony: Reduce clutter, especially in corners and on flat surfaces, to let go of things that no longer serve you; add water elements, such as blue and turquoise colors and a water feature to remind you to flow onward and move on.

84

EMBRACE THE HEALING TRIFECTA

Where do you go to relax and have fun? Many of us are drawn to regularly visit the ocean. There are specific reasons. Historically, cultures around the world have known, felt, and seen the health benefits of (1) the mighty ocean, (2) fresh, clean air, and (3) the warm sun. Doctors and other health professionals recognize it too. It is what we can accurately describe as the *healing trifecta*.

Have you ever visited the beach and seen bodies packed in everywhere with only tiny specks of sand to be found between them? I call it summer madness. It seems like fervent believers all flock to the same spots at the same time. Maybe they know something. Like a restaurant with great food, it's crowded because it's so good!

Being close to the ocean soothes us in ways that are difficult to articulate. Whether you live on a remote island in the Caribbean or the island of Manhattan in New York City, we can all learn to receive holistic health and healing using the concept of the healing trifecta.

Clean water, clean air, and sunshine are basic tenets of wellness. We can let the ocean waters heal us, absorbing and taking away our troubles. We can also fortify ourselves by using the positive energy of the sun to increase our emotional well-being and enrich our vitamin D intake through our skin. When we breathe in fresh, clean air, we are increasing and maintaining our well-being. In this way, the healing trifecta optimizes health while reducing stress and tension.

Did you know about these facts?

- Simply visiting the ocean and listening to the waves has been shown to reduce blood pressure, promoting relaxation.
- Water fountains have been found to be helpful when battling health problems, stress, and chronic fatigue. Some even say that listening to water is the best way to cure insomnia.

- Rainforests with waterfalls are particularly potent for peace and relaxation, because they combine the intense grounding aspects of the forest with the healing power of water.

Affirmation

> **I embrace the sea, air, and sun to heal my mind, body, and spirit.**

Holistic Prescription

Call to Action
Plan visits to the sea as often as possible and prioritize it as part of your healthy lifestyle.

Mother Nature
Use these herbs: lemon balm for physical restoration; chamomile for calming relaxation; and rosemary for purified physical healing love.

Gemstones
Activate these gemstones: blue agate for patience, peace, hope, and positive thinking; selenite for dispelling negative energy; and howlite for remaining true to yourself and to soothe emotions.

Feng Shui
For optimal feng shui balance and harmony: Use the healing trifecta at home and in your work spaces by adding water elements like circles, mirrors, and water fountains; use blue colors for optimal healing, relaxation, and letting go; do your best to plan visits to the sea to connect regularly.

85

GET GREEN

Some of us don't realize this, but…we need to experience natural green spaces every day. Yes, daily. More than just a pleasantry, we actually need nature to balance our moods to enhance our health, which increases our productivity and success.

Going for a walk is a healing experience. No special equipment is required. The trees and untouched beauty can promote calmness and peace in a way similar to the sea. Just look at green grass. It's soothing at the soul level. And it does not matter what kind of grass it is, or the height of the grass, or any other specifics. You do not even need to feel the grass to get some benefit. But hold on!

While simply looking at grass can do wonders for your disposition, physical connection is even better. Getting green and getting physical can be as simple as walking on grass. Do it as often as you can because it promotes stability; you will feel emotionally, physically, and spiritually grounded.

Walking on the grass works to calm and center yourself even more because, when you get physical with nature, your senses open; they become stronger and more immediate. Combining sensory experiences maximizes your benefit—for example, walking barefoot while feeling the bark on the trees, smelling the grass after it's been cut, or taking a hike during a nice downpour of rain.

To get this healthy benefit regularly, include as much greenery as you can in all areas in all your environments. Use fresh flowers and plenty of hardy plants that thrive indoors. You can take it a step further and paint your walls a beautiful green color. The color green symbolizes vitality and growth. It also represents money and prosperity, so you can't go wrong.

Affirmation

I see, touch, and feel nature every day.

Holistic Prescription

 Call to Action

Sit or lie on the grass as a way to meditate, get some rest, and even take a nap.

 Mother Nature

Use these herbs: green tea for physical body regulation; parsley for detoxification; and echinacea and elderberry to increase immune function.

 Gemstones

Activate these gemstones: jade for wisdom, peace, heart energy, and harmony; moss agate for increased immune functioning, happiness, and overall balance; and fluorite for peace and increasing mental clarity.

 Feng Shui

For optimal feng shui balance and harmony: Include all five elements (water, wood, earth, metal, fire) for natural balance; use metal and wood furniture, circular patterns, and purifying plants; hang artwork featuring green spaces, trees, flowers, the ocean, lakes, rivers, and other scenes.

86

RECEIVE HELP

Self-disclosure can help you heal. Reaching out can open up a world of possibilities. Some of us hold onto our guilt, shame, and negative past experiences out of fear. Fear of being discovered, fear of feeling bad, fear of judgment…

But the thing is…most people have a hard time keeping secrets. It's not natural. Our karmic divinity within seeks honesty, truth, and transparency. And sometimes we hit a wall. A plateau. A holding place where we are stuck. We know that we need to keep going and growing, but maybe we need help.

Don't be afraid to confidentially share your feelings with a trusted friend, advisor, therapist, or sisterhood support group. There are people here who can help you. Feel the weight lift as you are released from whatever may have happened to you and your feelings about it. Think about how that avoidance energy was taking up way too much space in your mind and body, affecting other aspects of your life. Then, poof! Let it go.

Everyone can get a fresh start at any time. You can receive help in getting healthy, maintaining emotional balance, and letting go of your past to move forward. Needing and accepting help shows great character, self-awareness, and strength. A lesser woman would have been defeated, but not you! Not only have you survived, but you also demonstrate more bravery by being able to let it go and chill out, choosing to expand your life instead of treading water like in the past.

Are you in need of assistance? Seek it. Like the waves of the ocean, it will come to you. But first you have to ask for what you need and know where to seek help. There are many resources available to you. See the Appendix for a list.

Affirmation

I am open to giving and receiving help in service to myself, my family, my community, and others.

Holistic Prescription

 Call to Action

Resist the urge to do everything yourself. Learn to delegate personal and professional tasks and develop your support system that includes those who can assist you in times of need.

 Mother Nature

Use these herbs: allspice for self-awareness, emotional healing, and luck; clove for physical stimulation and positive energy attraction; and thyme for spiritual awareness, plus healing with love and courage.

 Gemstones

Activate these gemstones: black tourmaline for higher elevated thinking; hematite for physical healing; and moonstone for self-protection and good fortune.

 Feng Shui

For optimal feng shui balance and harmony: Add earth elements and earth tones like beige for self-care and boundaries; add water elements like blue colors for increased connection, releasing the past, and wisdom; add wood furniture and green colors for healing and grounding.

87

AVOID THAT, USE THIS

In life, we learn what to use and what to avoid. For our purposes, this means what is healthy and what is not. Avoid stereotypes. Avoid denial. Avoid negativity. Avoid time sucks. Use knowledge. Use understanding. Use the time that you have wisely. Use the resources in this book.

There is no one "right" way to be healthy. So, let's be open-minded, yet clear about what we need. Know that a worry-free life of wellness is for everyone. Stop believing that it's only for affluent people or people of a certain race or religion! The diversity of nature is reflected in its people. There is no one color for holistic health—it is a fabulously inclusive blend of colors that always includes you.

Understand that anyone can heal. It is possible for you and everyone else. You can search your soul, reconnect to purpose, gain clarity and balance, feed your passion, and live a meaningful life.

Avoid judgments, especially when it comes to what helps. If it is useful to you, use it. Some people do breath work, coaching, yoga, travel, forgiving, screaming, therapy, isolation, journaling…but, ultimately, you have to do what feels right for you. Although some of the concepts in this book may seem a little strange to you at first, try to see the big picture and know that all of them are backed by science.

Stop pretending. And stop wasting time. It's not about needing more hours in the day. Do you make time for what you want? If not, it's okay, we all fall into this trap sometimes. But's let's try to avoid doing it again. The key is to prioritize and make time for only the activities that truly serve you. You are no longer in denial.

Being around people who weigh you down…who has time for that? Emotional vampires suck your time and attention to feed. When you starve them of time and energy, they shrink to nothing. Use this to your advantage and let them vanish.

Affirmation

> **I am open-minded and use what works best for me to achieve my health goals without judgment.**

Holistic Prescription

 Call to Action

Get real and stop swimming in the River of de Nile! Own what you do or don't do and the reasons why.

 Mother Nature

Use these herbs and flowers: allspice for self-awareness, emotional healing, and luck; jasmine for self-worth, beauty, and spiritual awareness; and thyme for spiritual awareness, plus healing with love and courage.

 Gemstones

Activate these gemstones: carnelian for strength, self-worth, and confidence; sodalite for getting in tune with your intuition and higher consciousness; and pyrite for transformative healing.

 Feng Shui

For optimal feng shui balance and harmony: Clear all clutter; balance the five elements (water, wood, earth, metal, fire) in your home; add metal furnishings, accents, and gold/silver/copper metallic colors to increase integrity and clarity; strengthen fire elements with white candles for meditation and relaxation.

88

PRIORITIZE THE VIBE

There is a Chinese proverb: "Tension is who you think you should be. Relaxation is who you are." Chilling out is the vibe.

Stop giving your power away by internalizing the negative opinions of people who do not know you. Don't allow their misery to become yours. Self-love is self-care. By not making yourself an important priority, you are creating a self-care deficit and blocking your blessings too. Life could be better. You can change the energy that you find yourself in by doing what you know you need to do to sweeten your life.

Energy moves. It also changes, and sometimes we are just *in it*. To err is human, but taking on too much is preventable. Yes, it is! Sure, you are finding your way, working toward emotional well-being with rest and calmness throughout your day. It's a balancing act, I know. But you can give yourself the loving guidance to make it better. Give yourself time and space to just *be*. Your heart and health will thank you.

When you prioritize the vibe, there will be more pleasure, compassion, understanding, comfort, and patience; less pain and negativity. It is exactly what many of us need at this moment. Always within you, the capacity to chill out is ever-present. Communicate it, be clear about it, and see how others respond. Chances are, they will respect it and want it for themselves too. Set the vibe every morning when you wake up and every night when you go to sleep.

Release doubt and fear! Fear kills the vibe. Don't let fear keep you from chilling out and reaching your full potential. Every morning, look into your bathroom mirror and recite this entry's affirmation.

Affirmation

Every day is a gift, and I use it as an opportunity to practice my chill.

Holistic Prescription

 Call to Action

Resist the urge to explain yourself or consistently act like you have something to prove. Chill out instead. Those who know you understand.

 Mother Nature

Use these herbs and flowers: lavender for peaceful relaxation and restorative rest; gardenia for expansive healing and peaceful self-love; and chamomile for calming relaxation.

 Gemstones

Activate these gemstones: aventurine for nurturing yourself, bringing joy, and a positive attitude; turquoise for health and inner calm; and larimar for stillness, calm, and chilling vibes.

 Feng Shui

For optimal feng shui balance and harmony: Clear clutter; add metal furnishings and pretty mirrors to increase love and beauty, peace and relaxation; choose your favorite colors that make you feel good and relaxed, for example—grays and gold/silver/copper metallic colors to include the water element; use gold as a royal earth color to inspire success.

89

CLEANSE

I admire your resilience and strength because it will always shine in begging for a new beginning. Some people tried to break you. Destroy you. Abuse you. Ignore you. Put you in your place. How dare they? They must not know about you! With resilience, you have the fortitude to take just about anything that they throw your way. And, over the years, they have been throwing it, I know.

Now, you bounce back stronger than ever. When you do, they are amazed. They are…bowing down with respect and admiration, wondering what your secrets are. One of your many secrets: cleansing.

Cleansing is more than cleaning; it is an overhaul and a way to balance yourself to "get right." Do you ever feel a need to press the restart button? Take it all and wash it away? Whenever you feel this way, you know it's your spirit telling you that it's time to reset. Time to cleanse.

That does not mean you will never have adversities again. Or negative experiences. Or enemies who disguise themselves as friends. But now you are more alert. Smarter, wiser, stronger, you also can recognize when it's time to start anew.

There are many ways to clean yourself up and neutralize a negative environment. For example:

- Try listening to ocean waves when you are tired or stressed to soothe and balance you.
- Taking it further, there's nothing like a soak in the ocean to instantly feel better.
- Use bath salts in your bathtub; Epsom salts, sea salt, and baking soda will also work.
- Burn frankincense, myrrh, and sage to cleanse yourself and your environment.
- Salt (sea salt, iodine salt) in the corners of a room can help clear negative energy in the space.

Affirmation

Like the waves going out to sea, I let go. Thank you, ocean, for taking away my challenges, losses, and difficulties. Thank you, sea, for cleansing me and letting me let go.

Holistic Prescription

 Call to Action

Most of us are more resilient than we realize. Our setbacks are temporary. As you cleanse, think of the many ways in which you are strong and capable of bouncing back.

 Mother Nature

Use these herbs: sage for spiritual purification and new positive beginnings; bay leaves for spiritual enhancement and protection; and rosemary for purified physical healing love.

 Gemstones

Activate these gemstones: smoky quartz for grounding and balance; aquamarine to clear the mind and connect to higher health and well-being; and unakite for removing negativity and balancing emotions.

 Feng Shui

For optimal feng shui balance and harmony: Clear clutter; add wood elements with plants and flowers for trust, healing, flexibility, and kindness; add earth elements with large natural furnishings for self-care; add water elements like water fountains and artwork of oceans, lakes, and streams to overcome challenges, let go, and bring in clarity and prosperity; visit the sea.

90

BURN IT

Did you know that you can hoard the past? Hoarding is a disease. Whether you hold onto physical items or past beliefs and experiences, you are still carrying unnecessary weight. This baggage is often a manifestation of fear, doubt, and the comfort of the familiar. Don't be a bag lady! It can trap you and keep you stagnant, like running in circles in the same spot.

Your body may be full of stressful disruptions caused by intense, rapid change. Negative memories lead to negative feelings. You don't need this! You can release the tension in your body once your mind releases it. Then your emotional balance can and will be restored. One way to accelerate your recalibration is to burn it to release it into the Universe, always and forever.

What Can You Burn?

- Herbs (see the Mother Nature section in this entry)
- Incense (sticks and resin)
- Paper (with details about what you want to release written on it; see instructions that follow)

Steps to Burn It Away

You can take great pleasure in burning that which no longer serves you. With this exercise, you can release your worries, emotional baggage, and old relationships by burning them away.

1. Take a sheet of paper and write down the aspects of your life that you want to release to the Universe. Be as specific and clear as possible.
2. When your list is complete, speak your list aloud by stating, "I release [whatever you want to release]" while burning the paper in a fireplace, fire pit, or other safe, fireproof container.

3. As the ashes disintegrate and blow away, visualize your issues fading and dispersing with the wind. Seeing the remnants of your burned paper disappear will set you free from the past.

Affirmation

As the fire burns my disappointments, fears, and painful past experiences, I am released to begin again, renewed and ready.

Holistic Prescription

 ### Call to Action
In completing this exercise, remember to be safe and practice fire safety with your activities.

 ### Mother Nature
Use these herbs: juniper berries for releasing negativity; cedarwood for positive new beginnings; and peppermint for enhanced healing, luck, love, and protection.

 ### Gemstones
Activate these gemstones: rhodochrosite for emotional healing from childhood trauma and reclaiming self; and unakite for removing negativity and balancing emotions.

 ### Feng Shui
For optimal feng shui balance and harmony: Add the fire element, such as red candles, pillows, and paint for dynamic energy and inspiration; add water elements such as a water fountain and the color blue to let go and neutralize fire.

91

ATTRACT PEACE

When you interact with people after reading this book, you will be able to clearly see who has learned to relax and let go and who has not. Most of the time, when we share space with people who are not managing their stress well or who have difficulties relaxing and letting go, their state of mind is contagious. In fact, their distress can escalate the stress response in you and those around you.

Anxiety and stress are situational and often personally defined. So is peace. You attract peace by being peaceful. You will attract peace when you and your environment are peaceful.

One of the best ways to attract peace is through nature exploration. When stuff goes haywire, explore! Go outdoors, visit a park, take a garden tour, and walk around the lake. While you are at the lake, watch the ducks. You may even see a few baby chicks or fish in the water. Notice the animals, insects, and life around you.

Maybe you are in your office or somewhere where nature is not readily available to you. In that case, focus on your breathing. By focusing on your breathing, and enjoying just being in the moment, it's likely that someone will ask you how you can remain so calm. When you explain your process of staying cool, calm, and collected, they may be shocked that an activity that only takes a few seconds or minutes can help so much.

When you take deep, intentional breaths and ground yourself, you are taking intentional steps to take care of yourself. It's smart. And attractive. Some might even find it sexy. Peace is sexy? Yes, it is. This is the type of energy that keeps bringing you opportunities to live in calmness, love, and light.

Affirmation

I easily attract peace by walking, talking, and acting in gratitude, constantly reminding myself of my blessings every day.

Holistic Prescription

 Call to Action

You may be tempted, but don't compromise your peace for anyone or anything. Remember how hard you work to find, attract, and maintain it.

 Mother Nature

Use these herbs and flowers: sage for spiritual purification and new positive beginnings; juniper berries for releasing negativity; and jasmine for self-worth, beauty, and spiritual awareness.

 Gemstones

Activate these gemstones: amber for soothing and inspiring a carefree, optimistic disposition; blue agate for patience, peace, hope, and positive thinking; and spinel to realign your life with hope, gratitude, and appreciation.

 Feng Shui

For optimal feng shui balance and harmony: Use earth colors like tan for grounding; add wood elements like furniture and plants to promote healing; add water elements like circles and blue colors for connection and peace.

92

WRITE IT AWAY

Young teenagers have it right when the instinct to keep a secret diary overtakes them. Were you that thirteen-year-old girl lying on your bed, scribbling feverishly in your diary? Maybe your first diary had a little brass lock on it. The lock probably made you feel secure in knowing that the deepest and darkest feelings that you were writing about were being kept confidential and protected, for your eyes only. Of course, who relies on just the lock alone? I bet you had a secret hiding place too.

Fast-forward to your life as an adult. On any given day or night, would I find you writing feverishly in one of your journals? It's a healthy habit. By journaling, you can write it all away.

Why journal? Journals are the ultimate form of self-expression. They contain your words regarding your experiences, your thoughts, your concerns, your dreams, and your feelings with no filter. You can fully exploit the freedom that a journal gives you to express who you are, what you feel, and what you want. Without social constraints or judgment, this is a rare kind of opportunity in your life to be your truly authentic self.

You learn so much about who you are and what you are becoming when you journal. Writing down your feelings, expressing your intimate thoughts to only yourself, exploring your deeper and darker selves in writing is therapeutic and often necessary for self-exploration and self-discovery. That's why *journal* is both a noun and a verb.

Journaling is therapeutic, because the act of writing and expressing is a physiological and emotional release, a way of literally letting go. And letting go is necessary, because it is how we are empowered to step away from our emotional baggage, past issues, and mistakes.

Journals document our learning curve toward progress and success. And they give us an opportunity to release so that we can chill.

Was there a time that you were not fully in love with yourself? You can also use your journal to affirm your evolution and to hug yourself, literally and figuratively.

Affirmation

I write in my journal to heal, love, grow, and prosper.

Holistic Prescription

 Call to Action

Writing negative experiences in your journal can assist with the healing process. Remember to always be open and honest with yourself in your communication.

 Mother Nature

Use these plants: thyme for spiritual awareness, plus healing with love and courage; juniper berries for releasing negativity; and lime to promote healing that prioritizes love.

 Gemstones

Activate these gemstones: lapis for wisdom and serene awareness; aquamarine to clear the mind and connect to higher health and well-being; and pyrite for transformative healing.

 Feng Shui

For optimal feng shui balance and harmony: Clear clutter; add fire elements by using fiery orange colors for inspiration; include green spaces and plants for healing purification.

93

MEDITATE FOR A NEW BEGINNING

Did you know that what your eyes visually see is already fifteen seconds in the past? Whether it's fifteen seconds or fifteen years, you have to let it go to start anew. Over the years, most of us have accumulated a bunch of excess baggage that causes stagnation. Knowing how to release it and open your mind to other parts of who you are will help. A lot. This is the key to a high-quality lifestyle. And how do we do that? By meditating.

Recall a time in your life when you were in a great place, in a very peaceful state of mind. Where were you? What did it look like? What did it smell like? Can you go there again? If you cannot physically go there, can you go there in meditation? When you learn how to "go there," you can do it anytime you need to relax and let go.

Using the power of meditation, you can embrace yourself to conquer any obstacles, including barriers to relaxation. When we can see those obstacles, we can remove them and replace them with something better. And, plus, you can travel!

You don't have to live on an island oasis, because you can go there anytime you want to, not just physically but by using meditation. In fact, why limit it to an island? You can go anywhere in your imagination. You can have one very special place or many.

To enhance your efforts even more, meditate at your Spot (remember, from entry 79: Find Your Spot?). You can also try the ancient practice of candle meditation (see the Call to Action in this entry). It is designed to help you let go of any issues holding you back from achieving complete peace. It is especially helpful for people who may have difficulties meditating.

Affirmation

I relax my mind, body, and spirit by making time for daily meditation.

Holistic Prescription

 ### Call to Action

Do a candle meditation. Sit on the floor or in a chair with a candle in front of you. Gaze at the candle flame for two or three minutes. Focus on the colors in the flame. Notice how steady the flame is and how it flickers. Close your eyes and visualize the candle in your mind. Relax and breathe while the candle soothes you.

 ### Mother Nature

Use these herbs: skullcap for releasing and relinquishing control; passionflower to reduce restlessness, anxiety, and insomnia; and lavender for peaceful relaxation and restorative rest.

 ### Gemstones

Activate these gemstones: lapis for wisdom and serene awareness; rhodonite for emotional clearing from shock, trauma, and emotional wounds to achieve balance, self-love, and self-compassion; and aquamarine to clear the mind and connect to higher health and well-being.

 ### Feng Shui

For optimal feng shui balance and harmony: Clear all clutter, to let go of things that no longer serve you; add the colors brown and yellow (earth elements) for grounding; use a small, wooden meditation table for growth and healing; add water elements, such as blue and turquoise colors, and a water feature for wisdom, connection, and a rhythmic, steady flow for meditation.

94

HAVE NO FEAR

We are evolving, and that can be quite uncomfortable. There will always be a reason not to do something when you are unsure of yourself, afraid, or paralyzed by fear. We might have a fear of failure, disappointing others, being judged, falling short of our own expectations, getting hurt, not being good enough, or unwanted attention—just to name a few. Sometimes we might even fear success.

So, first, ask yourself, "What am I so afraid of?"

Of course, it's difficult. That is why we often stay where we are, instead of pressing forward. The past is known, and the future is not. Why not go for it? You can conquer your fears and banish worry by confronting your inertia. Stop creating reasons why not, and focus on what you want. Stop asking "What if"; instead, say "When":

What if...	When...
my fish died?	I get home, I'll feed my fish.
I took that job?	I change jobs, I will get what I need.
they break up with me?	I get home, I am going to talk to them about my feelings in this relationship.

By saying "When," you focus on your potential. Maybe you can't see yourself. But others can see you. They see how brave, intelligent, and gifted you are. They are encouraged by your potential, maybe even intimidated by it. Even if you fall down, they've seen you get back up. They've seen you create a path where none existed. They saw you express your style in unpredictable ways. They were there when you loved, even when others were afraid or hopeless.

As you have gotten a little older, hopefully you realized that there is no time frame for your dreams; when you remove fear, there is no limit to what you can do or when you do it. Nothing can stop you except you. As you inch closer and closer to your goals, just know that you don't ever have to let fear hold you back. If it has before, it doesn't have to be that way anymore.

Affirmation

I am smart, bold, and fearless.

Holistic Prescription

 ### Call to Action
Expect all new ventures to have their own unique set of challenges. Surf the learning curve like a pro.

 ### Mother Nature
Use these herbs and flowers: allspice for self-awareness, emotional healing, and luck; jasmine for self-worth, beauty, and spiritual awareness; and clove for physical stimulation and positive energy attraction.

 ### Gemstones
Activate these gemstones: jade for wisdom, peace, heart energy, and harmony; kyanite for maximizing your full potential and uplifting self-expression; and tiger's eye for increasing confidence while releasing fear and anxiety.

 ### Feng Shui
For optimal feng shui balance and harmony: Clear all clutter; add round metal tables to increase joy and beauty; add fire with red candles for inspiration, passion, and action.

95

ELEVATE YOUR THOUGHTS

Are you working hard to smash glass ceilings and change the status quo? Attempts to marginalize you and your essence can take a toll. These macro and micro aggressions would most definitely adversely impact your mental health if you allowed them to. Let's focus instead on your liberation and joy. Elevate yourself with expressions of freedom in order to move to the next level of chilling out, relaxation, and letting go.

Elevating your thoughts is liberating, and mind elevation is the key to freedom. When you elevate your thoughts and move to the next level of personal transformation, you act with no fear. That is what freedom is about. Let me ask you this: In your life, right now, what makes you feel free?

You can find your freedom and experience it on a regular basis, no matter what. You have to, in order to survive. *You* own your femininity, your ethnicity, and your culture. Let it empower you.

Usually when people ask, "How are you?" they are met with a standard answer: "I'm good," or "Fine." However, is this truly the extent of your reality? How are you *really*? To find out, we must learn to listen beyond our thoughts and into our souls. Use the wisdom of your soul to elevate your mind and thoughts. Your sense of freedom is linked to your soul, not just your mind and body. This process of soul-searching will elevate your thoughts and enrich your life.

Reframe your thinking: Instead of focusing on loss, see a gain that has yet to be experienced. Instead of fear, embrace possibilities. Instead of absorbing negative energy, banish it. Think of your goals, then make them bigger and more expansive. Dream larger. Want more.

Affirmation

Today and every day, I embark on a quest of self-discovery, knowledge, and elevation.

Holistic Prescription

 Call to Action

Draw on the wisdom of your elevated ancestors to take the next step. They have your back.

 Mother Nature

Use these herbs: peppermint for enhanced healing, luck, love, and protection; clove for physical stimulation and positive energy attraction; and rosemary for purified physical healing love.

 Gemstones

Activate these gemstones: black tourmaline for higher elevated thinking; labradorite for intuition and to protect your aura; and kyanite for maximizing your full potential and uplifting self-expression.

 Feng Shui

For optimal feng shui balance and harmony: Clear clutter; bring in the outdoors by adding natural wood elements like tall plants and trees, large windows to see the foliage outside, and lots of green; add water and metal elements like silver and gold metallic colors and water features to go deeper to see and feel more; add fire elements in the form of candles, a fireplace, or fire pit to increase passion, inspiration, and dynamic energy.

96

OBEY YOUR SOUL VOICE

Firstly, you must hear your soul voice to listen to it, and then obey. It's a progression.

No matter how powerful your mind and body are, your soul is more closely aligned with your authentic self. It is more "you." There are moments in your life that will shake you awake and open up your heart. These are often crossroads in your life. You have to make a decision.

What does your soul voice tell you? What are you going to do?

Your soul voice tells you not just what feels good, but what feels right for you at this particular time. And…your soul voice can override the noise and distraction of your everyday life, if you let it.

Having such a powerful soul voice might not always be obvious. In fact, it may be hidden, waiting to be discovered. Who are you? What is your legacy? What is your karmic destiny? Spirit knows who you are and is excited about what you will become. Hopefully, you are excited too.

Our ancestors are the key. You are part of a vitally important cultural legacy of excellence. Find the powerful women in your family. They live inside you, directing and guiding you. Channel the courage, wisdom, and can-do spirit of your ancestors when you need it most. Through prayer, meditation, and even simple acknowledgment, we honor them. In the process, we honor our whole selves.

It is empowering to know that we are not alone. You are amazing. You have a story to tell. Stay true. Stay you.

Affirmation

Holistic Prescription

Call to Action

Guard your soul carefully. What you share with the world is only part of who you really are. Only those closest to you are very familiar with your true soul identity.

Mother Nature

Use these herbs and flowers: bay leaves for spiritual enhancement and protection; cinnamon for grounding and balancing energy; and jasmine for self-worth, beauty, and spiritual awareness.

Gemstones

Activate these gemstones: sodalite for getting in tune with your intuition and higher consciousness; pyrite for transformative healing; and peridot for positive energy, sunshine, and abundant blessings.

Feng Shui

For optimal feng shui balance and harmony: Clear all clutter; use earth colors beige, yellow, and orange for grounding; use water elements like circular designs to encourage natural flow, deep wisdom, and connection; add metal and fire elements with gold/silver/copper metallic colors and sunshine.

97

SEE YOURSELF MULTIDIMENSIONALLY

Look around you. Do those people know who you are? I bet they don't. Do you? There is often a disconnect between what we portray to those around us and who we really are. In that space, there is a lot of good stuff.

Born with blended, intersectional, multiple talents, identities, and paths, we can appreciate what a gift it is to be diverse. We can express ourselves with these divine powers. This is what freedom is all about. You are a blessing to the world. First, you need to know...

Know that you are more than what you do to make money. You are more than your position in the family. You are more than service to your community. You are more than somebody's something.

So interesting...so powerful. With more than just one gift, there is so much that you can do. By expanding and exploring the many facets of your identity, you are not ignoring your "main" self. You are simply acknowledging that role as one of many hats that you wear.

Living a great life means living multidimensionally and intentionally. Who says we need to just be one thing? You are special in the loveliest way, and no one is like you. Don't hesitate to express all of you, even those less popular thoughts, ideas, and opinions. Live life like no other. That's what makes the world go 'round.

Listen to that voice inside you. Yes, it's your soul voice! It's been telling you that there's more. More love. More money. More family. More life. More treasures. More treats. More stability. It's okay to want to be more, do more, expect more, and capture more meaning from your everyday life. You deserve it.

Yearn for expansion. Practice feeling worthy. Celebrate your wholeness.

Affirmation

> *I am a vibrant, multidimensional being. I express my gifts and talents every day in many ways.*

Holistic Prescription

 Call to Action

Think about when you became so one-dimensional. Explore what interests you to discover your passions and explore your hobbies.

 Mother Nature

Use these herbs and flowers: allspice for self-awareness, emotional healing, and luck; peppermint for enhanced healing, luck, love, and protection; and jasmine for self-worth, beauty, and spiritual awareness.

 Gemstones

Activate these gemstones: chrysoprase to help you recognize the grace and beauty in yourself; tiger's eye for increasing confidence while releasing fear and anxiety; and amethyst for fortification and increased spiritual awareness.

 Feng Shui

For optimal feng shui balance and harmony: Add metal elements like white, gray, and gold/silver/copper metallic colors to improve clarity; add fire elements like sunshine and red and bright orange colors to increase inspiration, dynamic energy, and confidence.

98

DO WHAT'S "RIGHT"

The best people always seem to do what's right rather than what's most profitable or convenient. What's right for you is not always going to be right for me. The choice is yours. Let's eliminate *should* and *have to* from our vocabulary. Because words have power. What are your powerful words?

Try *right*. Does it feel right? Right is not the same as good. Feeling good is not a requirement for growth or success. Sorry that your evolution is not always going to feel good, even if it's right.

What is "right" is unique to each person. Your soul and mind can uplift your body. What is right is what makes you feel your power. When you consistently do what's right, you optimize your health and happiness. You are empowered. Right encourages good karma, an individual, deeply personal aspect of our universal value system.

The Universe constantly invites us to do the right thing. It's about doing right by others, but also doing right by you, yourself, which means acting with self-respect. Every day we have multiple opportunities to define ourselves and redefine ourselves on our own terms. Imagine if we all did what was right, changed our priorities accordingly, and reconnected with our divine selves and each other…the best of me receiving the best of you… We can all do what's right together.

We are elevated to do the right thing when we:

- Consistently act with moral ethical fiber.
- Align our service to others with our priority for self.
- Do business and spend time with those of good character.
- Respect the honor system.
- Act with integrity.

Affirmation

Doing what's right for me comes naturally, even if others may not understand it at the time.

Holistic Prescription

 Call to Action

Gain courage to do the right thing, even when the consequences may be difficult or unexpected in the short term.

 Mother Nature

Use these herbs: bay leaves for spiritual enhancement and protection; thyme for spiritual awareness, plus healing with love and courage; and yarrow for protecting and raising the frequency of love vibrations.

 Gemstones

Activate these gemstones: apatite for willpower and strength through love; black tourmaline for higher elevated thinking; and fluorite for peace and increasing mental clarity.

 Feng Shui

For optimal feng shui balance and harmony: Add metal elements like mirrors to increase righteousness and integrity; add the water color dark blue for deep wisdom and connecting with the world; add a pink candle fire element for promoting loving energy and confidence.

99

MAKE IT OVER

Are there areas of weakness in your life when it comes to chilling out? Let's fix that.

We can start with beauty. When we chill out, we can stop taking the beauty around us for granted. Noticing beauty, spreading beauty, and becoming beautiful is loving energy and time well spent. Enhancing our home and work environments to be beautiful helps us love ourselves, heal, and achieve. We can enhance our entire lives with environmental makeovers.

Investing in your space is investing in yourself and your future. Your efforts can move you away from something that doesn't work for you toward something that works very well, with unlimited rewards.

These are some of the ways to "make it over" to maximize your positive, desired outcomes:

- **Bedroom makeovers.** Are you drawn to your bedroom? Are you easily exhausted? Oversleeping? Rest and sleep are underrated: When you lack good sleep, you are more prone to develop depression, diabetes, heart disease, obesity, and anxiety. At night, you can transform your bedroom into a moonlit slice of heaven to sleep and restore your body in peace.

- **Nature therapy.** Walk in nature when you want to and you desperately need a fix, and, as a last resort, technology can help you adapt using apps with nature images and sounds. When we lack nature in our lives, it is more difficult to maintain emotional balance, inner peace, and joy.

- **Office makeovers.** Whether at home or in a company building, if you spend significant time in an office, make sure it is a beautiful working environment that uplifts and inspires you, makes you feel good, and increases your chances of success every time you are there.

Be patient. Take your time. Be gentle with your process, knowing that there is no time frame or set of expectations when it comes to peace, healing, and elevation. Listen to Spirit when evaluating form and function. Healthful living looks different for everyone.

Affirmation

> **As I grow, my environment grows, too, in the most positive and healthy way.**

Holistic Prescription

 Call to Action

Use all five of your senses to fully appreciate the magnificence of your new environment.

 Mother Nature

Use these plants: rose for increasing love vibrations, including self-love; honeysuckle for beauty, personal power, and self-love; and lime to promote healing that prioritizes love.

 Gemstones

Activate these gemstones: aventurine for nurturing yourself, bringing joy and a positive attitude; lepidolite for attracting love, hope, and light, plus change acceptance; and turquoise for health and inner calm.

 Feng Shui

For optimal feng shui balance and harmony: Clear clutter; add the beauty of all elements; add metal elements by using gold and silver mirrors; add wood elements by including houseplants; add earth elements in your bedroom with soft sheets, and other soft, natural materials for yin soothing comfort.

100

MAKE YOUR HOUSE A HEALING HOME

Because our natural state is one of balance and equilibrium, if we are in tune with our environment, we can tell when something is not quite right, even if we can't put a label on it. Of course, we can tell when it feels very nice too. And these are the places where we want to visit, stay, and linger, so that we can absorb the good sensations.

A healing home is one that intentionally promotes your physical health, wellness, and emotional well-being. It is the ultimate safe place where you prioritize self-care. This means you can be yourself, chill out, restore, and renew here. It is an ideal space for achieving visual, vibrational, and spiritual balance. In addition to being safe, it is thera-peutic. It is in harmony with who you are and its geographical location.

Instead of being chronically stressed, think of ways that you can make your home an idyllic escape, one that makes it easy to have a more relaxed way of life. Knowing that every day is not guaranteed to be great, you always have your special space.

A healing home helps you manage stress; it doesn't increase it. Therefore, affordability might also be part of your process too. Improving your home in very specific ways with wellness intentions can and will improve your outlook on life and all conditions, not just your health. For example, your intrinsic power is waiting to be redis-covered with feng shui. With this ancient tradition, you can also find ways to increase finances, creativity, and career success.

As you grow, you will realize that healing is not a destination and peace is not a one-and-done process. Treat yourself gently with love and compassion. Learn to be your own best friend, lover, parent, and soul mate. And then, you will always feel at home.

Affirmation

I intentionally create a healing home that optimizes my holistic health.

Holistic Prescription

 ### Call to Action
Think of ways to ensure that your home is safe, therapeutic, and affordable.

 ### Mother Nature
Use these herbs and flowers: sage for spiritual purification and new positive beginnings; gardenia for expansive healing and peaceful self-love; and peppermint for enhanced healing, luck, love, and protection.

 ### Gemstones
Activate these gemstones: amber for soothing and inspiring a carefree, optimistic disposition; bloodstone for increased physical strength and vitality; and jade for wisdom, peace, heart energy, and harmony.

 ### Feng Shui
For optimal feng shui balance and harmony: Clear clutter; balance the five elements (water, wood, earth, metal, fire) throughout the home; invite a wellness specialist, such as a wellness real estate consultant, or a feng shui consultant to visit your home to make recommendations.

101

SPREAD THE CHILL

You can and will move permanently from worry to relaxation. Then, what else is there to do but spread the chill? Quite simply, a focus on relaxation can change the world. We can lead a movement, a project, an organization. But our culture shows us that we are never achieving alone. We are guided, protected, led, encouraged, accompanied, and joined by others.

Healthy people attract healthy people. Your massive team is ever-present with your ancestors, friends, mentors, colleagues, significant others, animals, and all organisms on the planet.

Of course, you can be more proactive. Your gifts are to be used. Failing to honor and use your talents means that you are not helping yourself or others. These are your gifts, your energy, and your life to squander if you choose to. But don't squander them, share them. *Please.*

An unrelaxed person is pretty easy to spot, and sharing space with them can be very unsettling, especially when we're already dealing with modern-day challenges like technology and pandemics. Many of us have learned that it's best to stay away from those people. This is advice that is useful for all ages in all circumstances, but you can't always live in a bubble.

Fortunately, being relaxed and at peace can be contagious. Relaxation is a dish best shared. We can heal ourselves and heal others by embracing a lifestyle of chilling out; each one can teach one. It is not just our choice but our duty and obligation to pay it forward, uplift each other, and mentor others in order to share the best of ourselves.

When we chill, we can be mindfully healthy, joyful, and peaceful together. A relaxed society is a healthy society. A peaceful community is full of promise and unlimited potential. In these spaces, we find care, love, friendship, prosperity, and abundance. I want to be there. Don't you?

Affirmation

> I am happy, healthy, and peaceful.
> I naturally share my joy with others.

Holistic Prescription

 Call to Action

When you see someone at the beginning of a road rage melt-down, help them by simply not reacting to their chaotic, uptight energy. Doing nothing, just maintaining balance and composure, can spread the chill!

 Mother Nature

Use these herbs: clove for physical stimulation and positive energy attraction; chamomile for calming relaxation; and rosemary for purified physical healing love.

 Gemstones

Activate these gemstones: blue agate for patience, peace, hope, and positive thinking; onyx for absorbing and transforming negative energy, plus increasing emotional and physical strength; and aquamarine to clear the mind and connect to higher health and well-being.

 Feng Shui

For optimal feng shui balance and harmony: Use earth colors like yellow for health and stability; add wood colors green and blue to promote relaxation and calm; add water elements like artwork with oceans and lakes and midnight blue colors for deep connection.

APPENDIX

Okay, you're here. You've read the book, every single page, and even bookmarked the most compelling pages with sticky notes. You studied it, discussed it in your book club, and have been reciting the affirmations every morning in front of your mirror when you wake up. You might be wondering, "Is this all there is?" Of course not!

The Art of Chilling Out for Women is designed to be a reference book that you can read and reread when the spirit hits you, when life inevitably changes, and when certain passages speak more to you now than they did before. This book is designed to be used. So, use it. Then use it the next day. And use it again after that. In fact, there is no need to stop. You can keep going to keep growing.

With any new lifestyle change, it's helpful to gather as many resources as you can, because they are important for success. There is still so much more to learn, experience, and do. Maybe you experienced difficulties with relaxation and chilling out in the past. You are not alone. You learned that each day is a fresh start. There are holistic, gender-specific, culturally relevant solutions waiting for you.

Like Mother Nature, resources for holistic health and well-being are so vast that they could never be contained in just one volume. However, reading *The Art of Chilling Out for Women* is a beautiful start and one that you should be proud of yourself for making. With that type of effort, your efforts will take you even further, if you want to continue this journey. Looking for more, absorbing more, and becoming more means you are putting yourself first and prioritizing self-care and self-development. It's something that you can pass on to your family, friends, and working community too.

Our most relevant learning tools are all around us. But to use them effectively, we need some discretion. This is where your deliberation, attention, and intention come into play. When you consistently have this mindset and move this way on a regular basis, it becomes a habit, and over time, quite simply, it is just the way you are. Then, you can begin to attract the resources you need to live the life that you want to live. Just like you found this informative book that is here to help, many more resources await you.

Besides yourself, like-minded people who can help you grow and manage yourself are tremendous assets, especially other women who embrace the spirit of sisterhood. There is great strength in finding your tribe and spending quality time with them. Authentic collaboration and rewarding partnerships are waiting for you! It can be much more engaging and fun than going it alone.

Resources

Organizations

Sisterhood Agenda: a nonprofit organization with a mission to educate, support, and empower women and girls around the globe; https://sisterhoodagenda.com/; (833) 3-SISTER.

Sisterhood Empowerment Academy (SEA): an oceanfront, eco-friendly learning space built on the island of St. John in the US Virgin Islands with relaxation, health, and healing programs and events for women and girls; www.seausvi.com/; (340) 714-7076.

Global Wellness Institute: a nonprofit organization with a mission to empower wellness worldwide by educating public and private sectors about preventive health and wellness; https://globalwellnessinstitute.org/; (213) 300-0107.

Psychology Today: the world's largest online portal for psychotherapy, offering access to hundreds of thousands of professionals; www.psychologytoday.com/us; (212) 260-7210.

American Psychological Association (APA): a national organization with a mission to promote the advancement, communication, and application of psychological science and knowledge to benefit society and improve lives; www.apa.org/; (800) 374-2721.

Meetup: a platform for meeting new people, learning new things, finding support, and making connections; www.meetup.com/; (212) 255-7327.

American Massage Therapy Association: the largest national community of massage therapists; www.amtamassage.org/; (877) 905-2700.

Books

Adams Media, eds. *The Book of Calm: 250 Ways to a Calmer You.* Avon, MA: Adams Media, 2018.

Adams Media, eds. *The Book of Happy: 250 Ways to a Happier You.* Avon, MA: Adams Media, 2018.

Afua, Queen. *Sacred Woman: A Guide to Healing the Feminine Body, Mind, and Spirit.* New York: Random House, 2001.

Balch, Phyllis A. *Prescription for Nutritional Healing: A Practical A-to-Z Reference to Drug-Free Remedies Using Vitamins, Minerals, Herbs & Food Supplements*, 5th ed. New York: Avery, 2010.

Benko, Laura. *The Holistic Home: Feng Shui for Mind, Body, Spirit, Space.* New York: Skyhorse, 2016.

Coleman, Angela D. *Girls Guide: How to Relax & Let Go.* Baltimore: Sisterhood Agenda, 2020.

Coleman, Angela D. *Life After ACEs: Overcoming Girlhood Trauma.* Baltimore: Sisterhood Agenda, 2019.

Gawain, Shakti. *Creative Visualization: Use the Power of Your Imagination to Create What You Want in Your Life.* Novato, CA: New World Library, 2016.

Grogan, Barbara Brownell. *Healing Herbs Handbook: Recipes for Natural Living.* New York: Union Square & Co., 2018.

Hạnh, Thích Nhất. *How to Relax.* Berkeley, CA: Parallax, 2015.

Kenner, Corrine. *Crystals for Beginners: A Guide for Enhancing Your Health, Intuition and Creativity Using Crystals and Stones.* Woodbury, MN: Llewellyn, 2006.

Myss, Caroline. *Anatomy of the Spirit: The Seven Stages of Power and Healing.* New York: Harmony, 1996.

Orloff, Judith. *Positive Energy: 10 Extraordinary Prescriptions for Transforming Fatigue, Stress, and Fear into Vibrance, Strength, and Love.* New York: Harmony, 2005.

INDEX

flexibility and, 102–3, 153
new beginnings, 21, 146–47, 162–65,
182–83, 204–5, 212–13
Chaos
anxiety and, 85
eliminating, 14, 88–89, 92–93, 102,
128, 174
internal conflict and, 85, 92–93, 174
protection from, 76, 128
Chilling out
benefits of, 9–21, 23–83, 85–151,
153–229
body and, 12–16, 23–83
mind and, 12–16, 85–151
Spirit and, 12–16, 153–229
spreading concept of, 228–29
Clarity, 30, 52, 102, 114–19, 122–23
Cleansings, 18, 60, 192–93, 204–5
Compassion, 42, 90–91, 138–39, 202, 226
Courage, 160–61, 164–65
Crystals, 19–20

D
Daydreams, 148–49, 184
Depression, 52–53, 180, 190–91, 224
Despair, 98–99
Diet, 68, 80–81
Disease
fatigue and, 17, 194
sleep deprivation and, 224
stress and, 13, 17, 26, 194
trauma and, 26
Distress, 13, 16, 23–29, 92–97, 102–3
Diversity, 200, 220

E
Elements, 20
Emotions
balancing, 140–41, 150–51
feeling, 52–54
trusting, 52–54, 124–25
Empowerment
benefits of, 40–41, 97–98, 119, 184–
85, 216–23
compassion and, 138–39
energy and, 40–41

Endorphins, 64–71
Energy
creative energy, 120–21, 148–49
heart energy, 38–39
love energy, 38–39, 78–79, 131
negative energy, 134–35, 158–60,
200–205, 216–17
positive energy, 52–53, 74–75, 94–95,
160–61, 186–95
reclaiming, 13, 40–42, 78–79
Energy centers, 20
Energy fields, 20
Essential oils, 18–19, 58, 61
Exercise, 64–65, 70–71
Exhaustion, 24, 40, 78, 88, 108, 172, 224

F
Fatigue, 17, 194
Fear. See also Worries
consequences of, 144–45, 214–15
courage and, 160–61, 164–65
of failure, 112–13, 214–15
identifying, 160–61, 214–15
processing, 164–65
releasing, 34–35, 202–3, 214–15
of unknown, 118–19
Fear of missing out (FOMO), 15, 133
Feelings
absorbing, 52–54
balancing, 140–41, 150–51
trusting, 52–54, 124–25
Feng shui, 20, 25
Fight or flight, 24, 26, 62
Flexibility, 102–3, 153
Flowers, 48–49
Forest bathing, 188–89. See also Nature

G
Gemstones, 19–20
Gratitude
absorbing, 13, 23, 52–53
for blessings, 52–53, 208–9
expressing, 52–53, 76–77, 81, 193, 209
Green spaces, 196–97. See also Nature
Grief, 76–77, 134–35
Grounding techniques, 15–16, 158–59

H

Harmony, 20, 25
Healing
    aromatherapy for, 17–18, 46–48
    crystals for, 19
    embracing, 194–95
    essential oils for, 18–19, 58, 61
    feng shui for, 20
    gemstones for, 19
    healing trifecta, 194–95
    herbal remedies for, 16–18, 58–61
    of home, 226–27
    journey for, 17–21, 30–31, 124–25,
        130–31, 138–43
    meditation for, 30–31
    nature and, 13, 17, 44–45
    relaxation and, 30–31, 228–29
    self-disclosure and, 66–67, 198–99
Healthy foods, 68, 80–81
Healthy lifestyle, 12, 52–53, 92–93, 130,
    174–75
Heart chakra, 42–43, 70, 78, 130
Heart energy, 38–39
Heart protection, 42–43
Heart space, 42–43, 78–79
Heartbreak, 38–39, 130–31
Help, receiving, 198–99
Herbal remedies, 16–18, 58–61
Herbs, 10, 17–18, 58–61
Hoarding, 206–7
Holistic attitude, 12–16
Holistic prescriptions
    call to action, 16–17, 21
    components of, 16–20
    explanation of, 11–19
    herbal remedies, 16–18, 58–61
    Mother Nature, 17–19, 48–51
    scents, 17–19, 46–48
Home, healing, 226–27
Hormone regulation, 45, 60–61, 64–65,
    123
Hugs, 38, 72, 130

I

Imbalances, 13, 174. *See also* Balance
Incense, 19, 58, 121, 135, 175, 204, 206
Inner peace
    attaining, 86–87, 128–29, 208–9
    choosing, 14, 154–55
    maintaining, 158–63, 174–75, 182–
        83, 190–91, 224–25
    tuning into, 92–93, 156–57, 168–69,
        180–89, 208–9, 228–29
Inner voice
    finding, 126–27
    intuition and, 118, 126–27
    listening to, 16, 118, 126–27, 166–69
    logic of, 166–68
    meditation and, 138–39
Intuition
    increasing, 116–18
    inner voice and, 118, 126–27
    listening to, 34–35, 116–18, 126–27,
        153, 166–70
    soul and, 153, 166–70
    third eye and, 116
Isolation, 72–73, 200

J

Journaling, 150–51, 174–75, 210–11
Journey
    healing journey, 17–21, 30–31, 124–
        25, 130–31, 138–43
    progress with, 122–23
    of self-development, 21, 52–53, 128,
        174, 230–31
    spiritual journey, 94–95
Joy
    absorbing, 13, 23, 52–53
    accessing, 190–91
    choosing, 52–53, 190–91
    prioritizing, 52–53, 190–91
    regaining, 134–35
    sharing, 228–29

K

Karma, 126, 130, 198, 218, 222

R

Relaxation
  breathing for, 30, 44, 74, 88–89,
    120–21, 162–63, 208
  healing and, 30–31, 228–29
  importance of, 9–10, 30–31, 34–35,
    228–29
  letting go and, 86–87
  restorative rest, 56–57
Resilience, 66–67, 96–103, 176–77,
186–87, 204–5
Resources, 230–33
Rest. *See also* Relaxation
  importance of, 56–57, 224
  restorative rest, 56–57
  sleep, 46, 48, 56–57, 66, 148, 224
Right, doing, 222–23

S

Sacred spaces, 42–43, 76–79, 138–39,
180–85
Safe spaces, 14, 138–39, 150–51, 168–69,
180–85
Scents
  aromatherapy, 17–18, 46–48
  benefits of, 17–19, 46–49
  body oils, 18, 58–59
  essential oils, 18–19, 58, 61
  flowers, 48–49
  incense, 19, 58, 121, 135, 175, 204,
    206
Self-acceptance, 28–29
Self-awareness
  body barometers, 13, 24–25, 70, 92,
    158
  increasing, 10–11, 46–47, 126–27,
    139–49, 160–65, 172, 198
  vigilance and, 40–41
Self-care
  beauty and, 74–75
  benefits of, 9–11
  for body, 12–16, 23–83
  grounding techniques for, 15–16,
    158–59

  prioritizing, 12, 42–43, 56–57, 78–79,
    106–7, 134–35, 160–61, 202–3,
    226–31
  protective shield for, 15, 160–61
  self-development and, 21, 52–53, 128,
    174, 230–31
  self-love and, 12, 16, 78–79, 90–91,
    110–11, 132–33, 160–61, 202–3
  self-preservation and, 16, 132–34
Self-criticism, 16, 118
Self-development, 21, 52–53, 128, 174,
230–31
Self-disclosure, 66–67, 198–99
Self-discovery, 10, 67, 124–27, 154–55,
210–11, 216–17
Self-doubt, 16, 124, 146–47, 202–3,
206–7
Self-esteem, 28–29
Self-exploration, 10, 126–27, 210–11
Self-expression, 17, 60, 142–43, 150–51,
210–11
Self-investment, 23, 32–33, 74–75,
224–25
Self-love
  embracing, 36–37
  heart energy and, 38–39
  nurturing, 178–79
  prioritizing, 42–43, 78–79, 106–7,
    160–61, 202–3
  proving, 36–37
  self-acceptance and, 28–29
  self-care and, 12, 16, 78–79, 90–91,
    110–11, 132–33, 160–61, 202–3
  self-esteem and, 28–29
  self-investment and, 23, 32–33,
    74–75, 224–25
  self-respect and, 110–11
  upliftment and, 68–69
Self-parenting, 90–91
Self-preservation, 16, 132–34
Self-respect, 110–11
Self-sabotage, 108–9, 178–79
Self-soothe, 76–77, 140–41
Self-talk, 15–16, 76, 138
Senses, 46–49, 72–73

Sex, 64, 66, 70
Sleep
    deep sleep, 56–57
    disease and, 224
    enhancing, 46, 48, 66, 148
    importance of, 56–57, 224
    restorative rest, 56–57
Slowing down, 17, 64, 80–81, 120–23, 162
Soothing techniques, 76–77, 140–41
Soul. *See also* Spirit
    intuition and, 153, 166–70
    listening to, 15, 126–27, 158–59, 166–75, 218–20
    logic of, 166–68
    nurturing, 15, 118, 178–79
    obeying, 158–59, 218–19
Soul logic, 166–68
Soul voice, 126–27, 158–59, 166–69, 218–20
Spirit
    activating, 94–95
    best interests and, 168–69
    body and, 12–16, 153
    chilling out and, 12–16, 153–229
    connecting with, 14–15, 153–229
    listening to, 15, 166–75
    mind and, 12–16, 94–95, 153
    power of, 153–229
    realigning with, 15
    trusting, 170–71, 174–75
Stillness, 82–83, 126–27, 176–77
Stress
    chronic stress, 26, 194, 226
    consequences of, 9, 13, 17, 24, 26, 34, 194, 226
    coping with, 34–35
    disease and, 13, 17, 26, 194
    relieving, 9–10, 56–57, 190–91, 208–9
Superpower, 82–83, 176–77
Survival strategy, 9, 24, 80, 184

T
Tension
    breaking, 62–63
    endorphins and, 66–67
    relaxation and, 202
    releasing, 9–10, 100–101, 162–63, 188–95, 206–7
Third eye, 116
Time-outs, 62–63
Touch, 38, 72–73, 130
Toxins, 45, 60, 68–70, 75, 81, 133, 197
Trauma
    childhood trauma, 92, 96–97, 114, 139, 207
    coping with, 66, 92, 96–97, 114, 139, 207
    disease and, 26
    releasing, 96–97, 192
Troubles, releasing, 92–93, 192–95

U
Unplugging, 40, 63, 132–33
Unwinding, 132–33, 154–55

V
Visualization, 42–43, 120–21, 148–49, 160–61, 184–87

W
Weaknesses, 160–61, 224–25
Workouts, 64–65, 70–71
Worries. *See also* Fear
    banishing, 34–35, 214–15, 228–29
    consequences of, 34–35, 138–39
    releasing, 9–10, 28–29, 205–7
Writing tips, 150–51, 174–75, 210–11

Y
Yin and yang, 20, 140–41
Yoga, 30, 64, 69, 156, 163, 200

ABOUT
THE AUTHOR

Angela D. Coleman, holistic health specialist and founder of the global nonprofit Sisterhood Agenda, has authored more than twenty books. She grew up in Newark, New Jersey, and graduated cum laude from Princeton University with an AB degree in psychology and African-American studies. Later, she studied clinical psychology at Howard University, earned a degree in nonprofit management from Duke University, and received an MBA from the University of Phoenix. She holds certifications in trauma, psychological first aid, suicide prevention, and African holistic health.